Iconites Air Fryer Oven Cookbook

Healthy, Easy & Delicious Recipes for Your Iconites Air Fryer Oven: A Cookbook

Fione Bornee

© Copyright 2020 Fione Bornee - All Rights Reserved.

In no way is it legal to reproduce, duplicate, or transmit any part of this document by either electronic means or in printed format. Recording of this publication is strictly prohibited, and any storage of this material is not allowed unless with written permission from the publisher. All rights reserved.

The information provided herein is stated to be truthful and consistent, in that any liability, regarding inattention or otherwise, by any usage or abuse of any policies, processes, or directions contained within is the solitary and complete responsibility of the recipient reader. Under no circumstances will any legal liability or blame be held against the publisher for any reparation, damages, or monetary loss due to the information herein, either directly or indirectly.

Respective authors own all copyrights not held by the publisher.

Legal Notice:

This book is copyright protected. This is only for personal use. You cannot amend, distribute, sell, use, quote or paraphrase any part of the content within this book without the consent of the author or copyright owner. Legal action will be pursued if this is breached.

Disclaimer Notice:

Please note the information contained within this document is for educational and entertainment purposes only. Every attempt has been made to provide accurate, up-to-date and reliable, complete information. No warranties of any kind are expressed or implied. Readers acknowledge that the author is not engaging in the rendering of legal, financial, medical or professional advice.

By reading this document, the reader agrees that under no circumstances are we responsible for any losses, direct or indirect, which are incurred as a result of the use of information contained within this document, including, but not limited to, errors, omissions, or inaccuracies.

Table of Contents

Introduction 6
Chapter 1: Iconites Air Fryer Oven Basics 7
    Iconites Air Fryer Toaster Oven Series 7
    The 10-in-1 Multipurpose Air Fryer Oven 8
    How the Iconites Air Fryer Oven Works? 9
    Cleaning and Maintenance 11
Chapter 2: 30-Day Meal Plan 12
Chapter 3: Breakfast Recipes 17
    Nuts & Seeds Granola 17
    Oats Granola 18
    Baked Eggs 19
    Eggs in Bread Cups 20
    Date Bread 21
    Cream & Cheddar Omelet 22
    Bacon & Kale Frittata 23
    Mini Veggie Frittatas 24
    Sausage with Eggs 25
    Eggs with Chicken 26
Chapter 4: Poultry Recipes 27
    Spiced & Herbed Roasted Chicken 27
    Roasted Spicy Chicken 28
    Spicy Chicken Thighs 30
    BBQ Chicken Wings 31
    Marinated Chicken Legs 32
    Glazed Chicken Drumsticks 33
    Breaded Chicken Breasts 34
    Buttered Turkey Breast 35
    Herbed Turkey Breast 36
    Garlicky Duck Legs 37
Chapter 5: Red Meat Recipes 38
    Bacon-Wrapped Filet Mignon 38
    Lemony Flank Steak 39
    Seasoned Rib-Eye Steak 40
    Spicy Beef Chuck Roast 41

Seasoned Beef Roast	42
Herbed Pork Loin	43
Glazed Pork Tenderloin	44
Seasoned Pork Shoulder	45
Herbed Pork Chops	46
Pork Stuffed Bell Peppers	47
Rosemary Leg of Lamb	48
Glazed Lamb Meatballs	49
Crusted Rack of Lamb	51
Sweet & Soup Lamb Chops	53
Lamb Burgers	54

Chapter 6: Seafood Recipes 55

Buttered Salmon	55
Lemony Salmon	56
Breaded Cod	57
Spiced Tilapia	58
Breaded Hake	59
Trout with Broccoli	60
Halibut & Shrimp with Pasta	61
Lemony Shrimp	62
Herbed Scallops	63
Crab Cakes	64

Chapter 7: Vegan Recipes 65

Brussels Sprout Salad	65
Basil Tomatoes	67
Spicy Potatoes	68
Almond Asparagus	70
Glazed Carrots	71
Spiced Zucchini	72
Sweet & Tangy Mushrooms	73
Spicy Butternut Squash	74
Lemony Okra	75
Seasoned Potatoes	76
Veggie Ratatouille	77
Tofu with Cauliflower	78
Tofu with Broccoli	79

Chapter 8: Snacks Recipes 80
    Spicy Chickpeas 80
    Mozzarella Sticks 81
    Tortilla Chips 82
    Feta Tater Tots 83
    Jalapeño Poppers 84
    Cauliflower Poppers 85
    Fish Nuggets 86
    Buffalo Chicken Wings 87
    Bacon-Wrapped Shrimp 88
    Crispy Coconut Prawns 89

Chapter 9: Dessert Recipes 90
    Banana Split 90
    Glazed Figs 91
    Lime Mousse 92
    Egg Soufflé 93
    Plum Crisp 95
    Fruity Crumble 96
    Zucchini Mug Cake 97
    White Chocolate Cheesecake 98

Conclusion 100

Introduction

A good and effective Air fryer toaster oven is all that you need to cook like professionals at home. The new convection toaster Air fryer oven series has been doing miracles for all the food lovers as these electric ovens can cook an endless variety of meals from crispy fries to roasted chicken and meat, desserts, snacks, breakfast, perhaps, anything that you would love to have on your menu. Iconites have launched its own series of Air fryer toaster ovens, and people who have seen this cooking buddy will second me on this that this electric appliance is amazing. It's not just the cooking functions that surprised me but the entire structure, the capacity, and efficiency, together make this oven a complete package for all. And just wait until you have the view of the classic 10-in-1 Iconites 20-quart Air Fryer toaster oven! It is surprisingly amazing. In this cookbook, you will find everything about these kitchen miracles, how it works, and, most importantly, how you can put to the use. A variety of recipes are shared in this book that will help you cook a great meal in your Iconites 20 Quart Air fryer Toaster Oven.

Chapter 1: Iconites Air Fryer Oven Basics

Iconites Air Fryer Toaster Oven Series

Iconites have managed to amaze its customers with yet another kitchen miracle, which has made Air frying, baking, grilling, roasting, toasting, dehydrating, and rotisserie all in one appliance, much easier than ever before. The Iconites Air Fry oven is the innovation of today that has successfully brought a variety of cooking functions in a single appliance. Imagine, instead of having an electric grill, a dehydrator, a toaster, an air fryer, and an oven separately lying in your kitchen, you will have one single appliance which can do all of that with much efficiency. This 10 in 1 multipurpose Iconites oven is extremely user-friendly and gives its users complete control over both the cooking time and temperature. This Iconites Air fry oven cookbook is designed to introduce all its readers to this digital oven, its features, and its better use.

The Iconites Air Fry oven is known for several of its advanced features and its ultimate benefits. Here are a few of its pros and benefits which make this Air fry oven a must to have for every household:

1. Family Size Space for Cooking

Unlike conventional oven or Air fryers, this Iconites Air Fry oven comes with a 20 quarts capacity, which means that you can have such a great room in there to cook a whole chicken, a turkey, and bake multiple things at a time. The 20 quarts capacity is great for large families and for people who love to organize parties every now and then; in this large-sized electric oven, you can cook a variety of meals to serve a number of people at a time.

2. All in One Machine

This Air Fry oven comes with ten functions in one. A user can Air fryer, Roast, bake, toast, dehydrate, and grill the food just on a press of a button. That's not just it; you get to choose from its given cooking presets to cook your favorite meals like pizza, shrimp, seafood, chicken, turkey, veggies, etc. You can also switch from one cooking mode to another during the cooking if needed. Besides these given presets, you can enjoy complete freedom of cooking at desired temperatures using its manual settings.

3. Energy and Time Efficient

Iconites is known for its energy-efficient technology. The device works on 18000 watts per hour, and it preheats quickly to reach the desired temperature. It only takes few seconds to Air Fry and bakes your favorite meal. The device also manages to keep the food warm until it is being attended.

4. Rich Accessories

This Air fryer oven comes with 13 accessories, including a skewer rotisserie, rotating basket, fry net basket, drip tray, 5pcs dehydrating racks, fetch rack, 2pcs oven mitts, chicken fork, Removable drip tray, and safe dishwasher parts, which makes cleaning super easy and cooking a breeze for even the beginners. These accessories are extremely user friendly.

5. User-Friendly

The Iconites Air Fryer oven has this extremely user-friendly control panel. It has a different button for its functions and a dial to switch between modes and increase or decrease the Time and Temperature. You get to have ten presets to choose from. All you need to do is to touch the given button, and the machine will automatically adjust its temperature and time.

The 10-in-1 Multipurpose Air Fryer Oven

The Digital Iconites Air Fry oven has brought such a revolution into the kitchen that now the users can enjoy fresh and crispy meals in no time. It is an electric oven that has merged with other Iconites features like the Air frying, broiling, toasting, and dehydrating. This appliance is especially good for people who love to bake and cook crispy food. The Iconites Air Fry oven 20-quart model is easily on its online stores, and this countertop convection oven comes with the following features and accessories:

- Iconites Digital Air Fry Oven
- 18000-watt unit
- Oven size and dimensions: 15.2 x 15.2 x 15.4 inches
- Dehydrating racks
- Rotisserie basket
- Rotating Basket
- Chicken Fork
- Drip tray
- Fetch Rack

- Mesh Basket

When you unbox the Iconites Air Fry Oven, you will find a rectangular unit with 15.2 inches x 15.2 inches x 15.4 inches. This unit has a front opening lid and control panel on the front. Inside the unit, there are side panels to insert the racks and place the sheet pan. The Air Fryer basket, pans, and trays are removable, and they all are dishwasher safe.

The Drip tray is placed inside and at the bottom of the oven to prevent the food and its drippings from falling on the oven base. This tray should be inserted for every session of cooking. The pan and racks are used for baking, broiling, or toasting. At the same time, the Air fryer basket is used to air fry the food evenly from all the sides. The different racks can also be used for baking, roasting, grilling and dehydrating purposes.

Its control panel displays the cooking temperature and time. The keys for time and temperature can be used to increase or decrease the values. You can adjust the values after selecting the required cooking operation or preset. There are keys to:

1. Switch on the light inside
2. Rotate the basket and rotisserie
3. Select the temperature
4. Change the cooking time
5. Select cooking presets
6. Switch on the Appliance
7. Turn on the Convection

The cooking temperatures can be adjusted from 180 degrees F to 400 degrees F, which means that you can cook it all without worrying about the temperature constraints. With the help of convection and rotating, you can ensure even cooking every time. The Air Fryer function of this oven is also quite effective as powerful hot air blown through the food, and it evenly cooks the food while passing through the net basket. Due to its large capacity, you can cook everything at once, and it saves a lot of your time since most other air fryer oven requires cooking in the batches.

How the Iconites Air Fryer Oven Works?

If you are having trouble using this appliance, then here are a few simple steps to make this device up and running.

Prepare the Device:

- First of all, check and look at all the components of the appliance and see if they all intact and in good shape.
- To use the appliance for the first time, clean or wash its cooking accessories like the baking pan, pan, and Air fryer basket and others, then let them dry completely.
- Now plug in the device and press the "Power button" given on the control panel.
- After pressing this button, the LED display will light up and indicate the device is one.
- Place its drip tray at the bottom of the oven. This tray is important to keep the oven base protected. Never forget putting this tray before every cooking session.

Mode Adjustments:

- The Iconites Air Fry oven quickly preheats itself, so it is recommended to place the food inside and then set the mode, time, and temperature accordingly. Or at least keep the food ready to place inside the oven when it is preheated.
- Place the prepared food inside and close the lid or door of the Iconites Air Fry Oven.
- To do so, first select the cooking mode. Simply select the desired preset given in the recipe. Remember, every preset has the time and temperature according to the type of food it is designed for. However, you can change it if your food requires more time or higher or lower temperatures. It all depends on the particular recipe you are using.
- After selecting the function, it's time to change the temperature and time settings.
- To change the cooking time, press any of the arrow keys given on top and bottom of the little "clock" icon given on the control panel. The upward-pointing key is to increase the cooking time, and the downward-pointing key is to decrease the cooking time.
- To change the cooking temperature, press any of the arrow keys given on top and bottom of the little "thermometer" icon given on the control panel. The upward-pointing key is to increase the cooking temperature, and the downward-pointing key is to decrease the cooking temperature.

Start Cooking:

- When the mode, temp, and time is adjusted, the device is ready to use.
- For Baking, Air frying, Roasting, Grilling, the device takes some time to preheat.
- The machine timer does not start ticking until the required temperature has reached. It preheats quickly.
- Once it is preheated, the device beeps to indicate that it will now automatically start

cooking, and its timer will start running.
- When the food is cooked, the device keeps it warm until you are ready to remove it from the oven.

Cleaning and Maintenance

Many of the users hesitate to buy large-sized cooking appliances because they are difficult to maintain and clean, but when you have the Iconites Air fryer oven, the users don't need to worry about that as this appliance comes with removable and washable accessories. The Iconites Air Fry Oven is designed specially to make cleaning extremely easy for all its users.

1. After every session, the device takes some time to cool down. Leave it for 15 minutes at least and allow it cool completely.
2. Unplug the device carefully as the appliance is cooling down.
3. Now remove all the removable accessories from inside the oven that may include the sheet pan, the wire rack, the Air fryer basket, and drip tray. Wash these removable items in the dishwasher or using the soapy water. Let them dry to use again.
4. Now wipe off the base of the oven and its exterior with the help of a wet cloth
5. Allow its base to dry out completely, then close it.
6. The device is ready to use again.
7. Insert the drip tray and other accessories to reuse the appliance.
8. Keep the appliance away from other heating elements and protect its powder chord from burning or heating.
9. Do not cover the vent of the oven with a cloth or anything. Keep it open for effective heating and cooking.

Chapter 2: 30-Day Meal Plan

Day 1

Breakfast: Nuts & Seeds Granola

Lunch: Pork Stuffed Bell Peppers

Dinner: Spiced & Herbed Roasted Chicken

Day 2

Breakfast: Eggs with Chicken

Lunch: Herbed Scallops

Dinner: Bacon-Wrapped Filet Mignon

Day 3

Breakfast: Cream & Cheese Omelet

Lunch: Brussels Sprout Salad

Dinner: Buttered Salmon

Day 4

Breakfast: Date Bread

Lunch: Almond Asparagus

Dinner: Glazed Pork Tenderloin

Day 5

Breakfast: Mini Veggie Frittatas

Lunch: Crab Cakes

Dinner: Buttered Turkey Breast

Day 6

Breakfast: Oats Granola

Lunch: Seasoned Potatoes

Dinner: Sweet & Sour Lamb Chops

Day 7

Breakfast: Bacon & Kale Frittata

Lunch: Glazed Lamb Meatballs

Dinner: Lemony Salmon

Day 8

Breakfast: Sausage with Eggs

Lunch: Herbed Scallops

Dinner: Rosemary Leg of Lamb

Day 9

Breakfast: Eggs in Bread Cups

Lunch: Pork Stuffed Bell Peppers

Dinner: Spicy Chicken Thighs

Day 10

Breakfast: Baked Eggs

Lunch: Beans & Veggie Burgers

Dinner: Lemony Flank Steak

Day 11

Breakfast: Eggs with Chicken

Lunch: Glazed Lamb Meatballs

Dinner: Trout with Broccoli

Day 12

Breakfast: Date Bread

Lunch: Spicy Potatoes

Dinner: Seasoned Beef Roast

Day 13

Breakfast: Cream & Cheese Omelet

Lunch: Tofu with Broccoli

Dinner: Spiced Tilapia

Day 14

Breakfast: Mini Veggie Frittatas

Lunch: Lamb Burgers

Dinner: Herbed Pork Loin

Day 15

Breakfast: Baked Eggs

Lunch: Lemony Shrimp

Dinner: Crusted Rack of Lamb

Day 16

Breakfast: Oats Granola

Lunch: Brussels Sprout Salad

Dinner: Crusted Rack of Lamb

Day 17

Breakfast: Sausage with Eggs

Lunch: Spiced Zucchini

Dinner: Breaded Hake

Day 18

Breakfast: Bacon & Kale Frittata

Lunch: Seasoned Potatoes

Dinner: Breaded Chicken Breasts

Day 19

Breakfast: Eggs in Bread Cups

Lunch: Crab Cakes

Dinner: Herbed Pork Chops

Day 20

Breakfast: Baked Eggs

Lunch: Pork Stuffed Bell Peppers

Dinner: Herbed Turkey Breast

Day 21

Breakfast: Nuts & Seeds Granola

Lunch: Lemony Okra

Dinner: Glazed Pork Tenderloin

Day 22

Breakfast: Bacon & Kale Frittata

Lunch: Herbed Scallops

Dinner: garlicky duck Legs

Day 23

Breakfast: Cream & Cheese Omelet

Lunch: Lamb Burgers

Dinner: Halibut & Shrimp with Pasta

Day 24

Breakfast: Date Bread

Lunch: Tofu in Orange Sauce

Dinner: Seasoned Rib0Eye Steak

Day 25

Breakfast: Sausage with Eggs

Lunch: Beans & Veggie Burgers

Dinner: Glazed Chicken Drumsticks

Day 26

Breakfast: Oats Granola

Lunch: Crab Cakes

Dinner: Spicy Beef Chuck Roast

Day 27

Breakfast: Mini Veggie Frittatas

Lunch: Sweet & Tangy Mushrooms

Dinner: Roasted Spicy Chicken

Day 28

Breakfast: Eggs in Bread Cups

Lunch: Lemony Shrimp

Dinner: Seasoned Pork Shoulder

Day 29

Breakfast: Eggs with Chicken

Lunch: Spiced Zucchini

Dinner: Lemony Salmon

Day 30

Breakfast: Nuts & Seeds Granola

Lunch: Lamb Burgers

Dinner: Marinated Chicken Legs

Chapter 3: Breakfast Recipes

Nuts & Seeds Granola

Preparation Time: 15 minutes
Cooking Time: 15 minutes
Servings: 8

Ingredients:

- 1/3 cup canola oil
- ¼ cup maple syrup
- 2 tablespoons honey
- ½ teaspoon vanilla extract
- 2 cups rolled oats
- ½ cup wheat germ, toasted
- ¼ cup dried cherries
- ¼ cup dried blueberries
- 2 tablespoons dried cranberries
- 2 tablespoons sunflower seeds
- 2 tablespoons pumpkin seeds, shelled
- 1 tablespoon flaxseed
- 2 tablespoons pecans, chopped
- 2 tablespoons hazelnuts, chopped
- 2 tablespoons almonds, chopped
- 2 tablespoons walnuts, chopped
- ½ teaspoon ground cinnamon

Method:

1. In a small bowl, add the oil and maple syrup and mix well.
2. In a large bowl, add the remaining ingredients and mix well.
3. Add the oil mixture and mix until well combined.
4. Place the mixture into a baking dish that will fit in the Iconites Air Fryer Oven.
5. Select "Air Fry" of Iconites Air Fryer Toaster Oven and then adjust the temperature to 350 degrees F.
6. Set the timer for 15 minutes and press "Start" to preheat.
7. After preheating, insert the baking dish in the center position of oven.
8. Stir the granola after every 5 minutes.
9. When cooking time is complete, remove the baking dish from oven.
10. Set the granola side to cool completely before serving.

Nutritional Information per Serving:

- Calories 302
- Total Fat 16.1 g
- Saturated Fat 2.1 g
- Cholesterol 0 mg
- Sodium 4 mg
- Total Carbs 35.1 g
- Fiber 5.7 g
- Sugar 14 g
- Protein 6.9 g

Oats Granola

Preparation Time: 15 minutes
Cooking Time: 15 minutes
Servings: 8

Ingredients:

- 1/3 cup butter, melted
- 1/3 cup honey
- ½ teaspoon pure vanilla extract
- 2 cups rolled oats
- ½ cup wheat germ, toasted
- ½ cup plus 2 tablespoons dried cranberries
- 4 tablespoons pumpkin seeds, shelled
- 1 tablespoon flax seed
- ½ cup walnuts, chopped
- ½ teaspoon ground cinnamon

Method:

1. In a small bowl, add the butter and honey and mix well.
2. In a large bowl, add the remaining ingredients and mix well.
3. Add the butter mixture and mix until well combined.
4. Place the mixture into a baking dish that will fit in the Iconites Air Fryer Oven.
5. Select "Air Fry" of Iconites Air Fryer Oven and then adjust the temperature to 350 degrees F.
6. Set the timer for 15 minutes and press "Start" to preheat.
7. After preheating, insert the baking dish in the center position of oven.
8. When cooking time is complete, remove the baking dish from oven.
9. Set the granola side to cool completely before serving.

Nutritional Information per Serving:

- Calories 297
- Total Fat 16.6 g
- Saturated Fat 5.9 g
- Cholesterol 20 mg
- Sodium 58 mg
- Total Carbs 31.7 g
- Fiber 4.5 g
- Sugar 12.8 g
- Protein 8 g

Baked Eggs

Preparation Time: 10 minutes
Cooking Time: 12 minutes
Servings: 4

Ingredients:

- 1 cup marinara sauce, divided
- 1 tablespoon capers, drained and divided
- 8 eggs
- ¼ cup whipping cream, divided
- ¼ cup Parmesan cheese, shredded and divided
- Salt and ground black pepper, as required

Method:

1. Grease 4 ramekins. Set aside.
2. Divide the marinara sauce in the bottom of each prepared ramekin evenly and top with capers.
3. Carefully, crack 2 eggs over marinara sauce into each ramekin and top with cream, followed by the Parmesan cheese.
4. Sprinkle each ramekin with salt and black pepper.
5. Select "Bake" of Iconites Air Fryer Oven and then adjust the temperature to 400 degrees F.
6. Set the timer for 12 minutes and press "Start" to preheat.
7. After preheating, arrange the ramekins over the wire rack and insert in the oven.
8. When cooking time is complete, remove the ramekins from oven.
9. Serve warm.

Nutritional Information per Serving:

- Calories 223
- Total Fat 14.1 g
- Saturated Fat 5.5 g
- Cholesterol 341 mg
- Sodium 569 mg
- Total Carbs 9.8 g
- Fiber 1.7 g
- Sugar 6.2 g
- Protein 14.3 g

Eggs in Bread Cups

Preparation Time: 10 minutes
Cooking Time: 23 minutes
Servings: 4

Ingredients:

- 4 bacon slices
- 2 bread slices, crust removed
- 4 eggs
- Salt and ground black pepper, as required

Method:

1. Grease 4 cups of muffin tin and set aside.
2. Heat a small frying pan over medium-high heat and cook the bacon slices for about 2-3 minutes.
3. With a slotted spoon, transfer the bacon slice onto a paper towel-lined plate to cool.
4. Break each bread slice in half.
5. Arrange 1 bread slices half in each of prepared muffin cup and press slightly.
6. Now, arrange 1 bacon slice over each bread slice in a circular shape.
7. Crack 1 egg into each muffin cup and sprinkle with salt and black pepper.
8. Select "Bake" of Iconites Air Fryer Oven and then adjust the temperature to 350 degrees F.
9. Set the timer for 20 minutes and press "Start" to preheat.
10. After preheating, arrange the muffin tin over the wire rack and insert in the oven.
11. When cooking time is complete, remove the muffin tin from oven.
12. Serve warm.

Nutritional Information per Serving:

- Calories 98
- Total Fat 6.6 g
- Saturated Fat 2.1 g
- Cholesterol 168 mg
- Sodium 206 mg
- Total Carbs 2.6 g
- Fiber 0.1 g
- Sugar 0.5 g
- Protein 7.3 g

Date Bread

Preparation Time: 15 minutes
Cooking Time: 22 minutes
Servings: 10

Ingredients:

- 2½ cups dates, pitted and chopped
- ¼ cup butter
- 1 cup hot water
- 1½ cups flour
- ½ cup brown sugar
- 1 teaspoon baking powder
- 1 teaspoon baking soda
- ½ teaspoon salt
- 1 egg

Method:

1. In a large bowl, add the dates, butter and top with the hot water.
2. Set aside for about 5 minutes.
3. In a separate bowl, mix together the flour, brown sugar, baking powder, baking soda and salt.
4. In the bowl of dates, add the flour mixture and egg and mix well.
5. Place the mixture into a greased baking pan.
6. Select "Air Fry" of Iconites Air Fryer Oven and then adjust the temperature to 340 degrees F.
7. Set the timer for 22 minutes and press "Start" to preheat.
8. After preheating, arrange the baking pan over the wire rack and insert in the oven.
9. When cooking time is complete, remove the pan from oven and place the pan onto a wire rack for about 10-15 minutes.
10. Carefully, invert the bread onto the wire rack to cool completely before slicing.
11. Cut the bread into desired size slices and serve.

Nutritional Information per Serving:

- Calories 269
- Total Fat 5.4 g
- Saturated Fat 3.1 g
- Cholesterol 29 mg
- Sodium 285 mg
- Total Carbs 55.1 g
- Fiber 64.1 g
- Sugar 35.3 g
- Protein 3.6 g

Cream & Cheddar Omelet

Preparation Time: 10 minutes
Cooking Time: 8 minutes
Servings: 2

Ingredients:

- 4 eggs
- ¼ cup cream
- Salt and ground black pepper, as required
- ¼ cup Cheddar cheese, grated

Method:

1. In a bowl, add the eggs, cream, salt, and black pepper and beat until well combined.
2. Place the egg mixture into a small baking pan.
3. Select "Air Fry" of Iconites Air Fryer Oven and then adjust the temperature to 350 degrees F.
4. Set the timer for 8 minutes and press "Start" to preheat.
5. After preheating, arrange the baking pan over the wire rack and insert in the oven.
6. After 4 minutes, sprinkle the omelet with cheese evenly.
7. When cooking time is complete, remove the baking pan from oven.
8. Cut the omelette into 2 portions and serve hot.

Nutritional Information per Serving:

- Calories 88
- Total Fat 15.1 g
- Saturated Fat 6.8 g
- Cholesterol 348 mg
- Sodium 298 mg
- Total Carbs 1.8 g
- Fiber 0 g
- Sugar 1.4 g
- Protein 14.8 g

Bacon & Kale Frittata

Preparation Time: 15 minutes
Cooking Time: 16 minutes
Servings: 2

Ingredients:

- ¼ cup bacon, chopped
- ¼ cup fresh kale, tough ribs removed and chopped
- ½ of tomato, cubed
- 3 eggs
- Salt and ground black pepper, as required
- ¼ cup Parmesan cheese, grated

Method:

1. Heat a nonstick skillet over medium heat and cook the bacon for about 5 minutes.
2. Add the kale and cook for about 1-2 minutes.
3. Add the tomato and cook for about 2-3 minutes.
4. Remove from the heat and drain the grease from skillet.
5. Set aside to cool slightly.
6. Meanwhile, in a small bowl, add the eggs, salt and black pepper and beat well.
7. In a greased baking dish, place the bacon mixture and top with the eggs, followed by the cheese.
8. Select "Air Fry" of Iconites Air Fryer Oven and then adjust the temperature to 355 degrees F.
9. Set the timer for 8 minutes and press "Start" to preheat.
10. After preheating, arrange the baking dish in the center of oven.
11. When cooking time is complete, remove the baking dish from oven.
12. Cut into equal-sized wedges and serve.

Nutritional Information per Serving:

- Calories 293
- Total Fat 19.7 g
- Saturated Fat 9.8 g
- Cholesterol 279 mg
- Sodium 935 mg
- Total Carbs 3.4 g
- Fiber 0.3 g
- Sugar 0.9 g
- Protein 25.4 g

Mini Veggie Frittatas

Preparation Time: 15 minutes
Cooking Time: 17 minutes
Servings: 2

Ingredients:

- 1 tablespoon butter
- ½ of white onion, sliced thinly
- 1 cup fresh mushrooms, sliced thinly
- 1¼ cups fresh spinach, chopped
- 3 eggs
- ½ teaspoon fresh rosemary, chopped
- Salt and ground black pepper, as required
- 3 tablespoons Parmesan cheese, shredded

Method:

1. In a frying pan, melt butter over medium heat and cook the onion and mushroom for about 3 minutes.
2. Add the spinach and cook for about 2-3 minutes.
3. Remove the frying pan from heat and set aside to cool slightly.
4. Meanwhile, in a small bowl, add the eggs, rosemary, salt and black pepper and beat well.
5. Divide the beaten eggs in 2 greased ramekins evenly and top with the veggie mixture, followed by the cheese.
6. Select "Air Fry" of Iconites Air Fryer Oven and then adjust the temperature to 330 degrees F.
7. Set the timer for 12 minutes and press "Start" to preheat.
8. After preheating, place the ramekins over the rack and insert in the oven.
9. When cooking time is complete, remove the ramekins from oven and place onto a wire rack for about 5 minutes before serving.

Nutritional Information per Serving:

- Calories 200
- Total Fat 14.6 g
- Saturated Fat 7 g
- Cholesterol 266 mg
- Sodium 356 mg
- Total Carbs 5.4 g
- Fiber 1.5 g
- Sugar 2.4 g
- Protein 13.2 g

Sausage with Eggs

Preparation Time: 10 minutes
Cooking Time: 6 minutes
Servings: 2

Ingredients:

- 4 breakfast sausage
- 2 hard-boiled eggs, peeled
- 1 avocado, peeled, pitted and sliced

Method:

1. Arrange the sausages in the rotisserie basket and attach the lid.
2. Arrange the drip pan in the bottom of Instant Iconites Air Fryer Oven cooking chamber.
3. Select "Roast" of Iconites Air Fryer Oven and then adjust the temperature to 375 degrees F.
4. Set the timer for 6 minutes and press "Start" to preheat.
5. After preheating, arrange the rotisserie basket, on the rotisserie spit.
6. Then, close the door and touch "Rotate".
7. When cooking time is complete, press the red lever to release the rod.
8. Remove from the oven and place the sausages onto serving plates.
9. Divide eggs and avocado slices onto each plate and serve.

Nutritional Information per Serving:

- Calories 322
- Total Fat 28.5 g
- Saturated Fat 6.9 g
- Cholesterol 177 mg
- Sodium 187 mg
- Total Carbs 9 g
- Fiber 6.7 g
- Sugar 0.8 g
- Protein 10.6 g

Eggs with Chicken

Preparation Time: 15 minutes
Cooking Time: 12 minutes
Servings: 3

Ingredients:

- 4 large eggs, divided
- 2 tablespoons heavy cream
- Salt and ground black pepper, as required
- 2 teaspoons unsalted butter, softened
- 2 ounces cooked chicken, chopped
- 3 tablespoons Parmesan cheese, grated finely
- 2 teaspoons fresh parsley, minced

Method:

1. In a bowl, add 1 egg, cream, salt and black pepper and beat until smooth.
2. In the bottom of a pie pan, place the butter and spread evenly.
3. In the bottom of pie pan, place chicken over butter and top with the egg mixture evenly.
4. Carefully, crack the remaining eggs on top.
5. Sprinkle with salt and black pepper and top with cheese and parsley evenly.
6. Select "Air Fry" of Iconites Air Fryer Oven and then adjust the temperature to 320 degrees F.
7. Set the timer for 12 minutes and press "Start" to preheat.
8. After preheating, arrange pan over the wire rack and insert in the oven.
9. When cooking time is complete, remove the pan from oven.
10. Cut into equal-sized wedges and serve hot.

Nutritional Information per Serving:

- Calories 199
- Total Fat 14.7 g
- Saturated Fat 6.7 g
- Cholesterol 287 mg
- Sodium 221 mg
- Total Carbs 0.8 g
- Fiber 0 g
- Sugar 0.5 g
- Protein 16.1 g

Chapter 4: Poultry Recipes

Spiced & Herbed Roasted Chicken

Preparation Time: 15 minutes
Cooking Time: 1 hour
Servings: 8

Ingredients:

- 1 teaspoon dried thyme, crushed
- 1 teaspoon dried rosemary, crushed
- 1 teaspoon dried oregano, crushed
- 2 teaspoons paprika
- 1 teaspoon ground cumin
- 1 teaspoon garlic powder
- Salt and ground black pepper, as required
- 1 (4½-pound) whole chicken, necks and giblets removed
- 3 tablespoons olive oil, divided

Method:

1. In a bowl, mix together the herbs, spices, salt and black pepper.
2. Coat the chicken with 2 tablespoons of oil and then, rub inside, outside and underneath the skin with half of the herb mixture generously.
3. Arrange the chicken into the greased basket, breast-side down.
4. Select "Air Fry" of Iconites Air Fryer Oven and then adjust the temperature to 360 degrees F.
5. Set the timer for 60 minutes and press "Start" to preheat.
6. After preheating, insert the basket in the center position of oven.
7. Flip the chicken once halfway through.
8. Coat the chicken with the remaining oil and then, rub with the remaining herb mixture.
9. When cooking time is complete, remove the basket from oven.
10. Place the chicken onto a platter for about 5-10 minutes before carving.
11. With a sharp knife, cut the chicken into desired sized pieces and serve.

Nutritional Information per Serving:

- Calories 435
- Total Fat 213.26.6 g
- Saturated Fat 3 g
- Cholesterol 196 mg
- Sodium 181 mg
- Total Carbs 1 g
- Fiber 0.5 g
- Sugar 0.2 g
- Protein 74.2 g

Roasted Spicy Chicken

Preparation Time: 10 minutes
Cooking Time: 40 minutes
Servings: 4

Ingredients:

- 1 teaspoon dried oregano
- 1 teaspoon dried rosemary
- 1 teaspoon paprika
- 1 teaspoon garlic powder
- Salt and ground black pepper, as required
- 1 (3-pound) whole chicken, neck and giblets removed
- 1 lemon, quartered
- 3 garlic cloves, halved
- 2 fresh rosemary sprigs
- 2 tablespoons olive oil

Method:

1. In a small bowl, mix together the dried herbs, spices, salt and black pepper.
2. Stuff the chicken cavity with lemon, garlic, and rosemary sprigs.
3. With kitchen twine, tie the chicken.
4. Coat the chicken with oil evenly and then, rub with the herb mixture.
5. Insert the rotisserie rod through the chicken.
6. Insert the rotisserie forks, one on each side of the rod to secure the rod to the chicken.
7. Arrange the drip pan in the bottom of Instant Iconites Air Fryer Oven cooking chamber.
8. Select "Roast" of Iconites Air Fryer Oven and then adjust the temperature to 375 degrees F.
9. Set the timer for 40 minutes and press "Start" to preheat.
10. After preheating, press the red lever down and load the left side of the rod into the oven.
11. Now, slide the rod's left side into the groove along the metal bar so it doesn't move.
12. Then, close the door and touch "Rotate".
13. When cooking time is complete, press the red lever to release the rod.
14. Remove from the oven and place the chicken onto a platter for about 5-10 minutes before carving.
15. With a sharp knife, cut the chicken into desired sized pieces and serve.

Nutritional Information per Serving:

- Calories 584
- Total Fat 17.5 g
- Saturated Fat 3.9 g
- Cholesterol 262 mg
- Sodium 254 mg
- Total Carbs 2.3 g
- Fiber 0.7 g
- Sugar 0.4 g
- Protein 99 g

Spicy Chicken Thighs

Preparation Time: 15 minutes
Cooking Time: 20 minutes
Servings: 4

Ingredients:

- 4 (4-ounces) skinless, boneless chicken thighs
- ½ teaspoon cayenne pepper
- ½ teaspoon paprika
- ½ teaspoon ground cumin
- Salt and ground black pepper, as required
- 2 tablespoons olive oil

Method:

1. In a bowl, mix together the spices, salt and black pepper.
2. Rub the chicken thighs with spice mixture evenly and then, brush with melted butter.
3. Place the chicken thighs into a greased baking pan.
4. Arrange the drip pan in the bottom of Iconites Air Fryer Oven.
5. Place the baking pan over the drip pan.
6. Select "Bake" of Iconites Air Fryer Oven and then adjust the temperature to 450 degrees F.
7. Set the timer for 20 minutes and press "Start" to preheat.
8. After preheating, place the baking pan over the drip pan.
9. When cooking time is complete, remove the pan from oven.
10. Serve hot.

Nutritional Information per Serving:

- Calories 204
- Total Fat 11.2 g
- Saturated Fat 2.5 g
- Cholesterol 66 mg
- Sodium 80 mg
- Total Carbs 0.4 g
- Fiber 0.2 g
- Sugar 0.1 g
- Protein 25.4 g

BBQ Chicken Wings

Preparation Time: 20 minutes
Cooking Time: 25 minutes
Servings: 4

Ingredients:

- 2 pounds chicken wingettes and drumettes
- ½ cup ketchup
- 3 tablespoons white vinegar
- 2 tablespoons honey
- 2 tablespoons molasses
- ½ teaspoon liquid smoke
- ¼ teaspoon paprika
- ¼ teaspoon garlic powder
- Pinch of cayenne pepper

Method:

1. Arrange the wings onto 2 cooking trays in a single layer.
2. Arrange the drip pan in the bottom of Instant Iconites Air Fryer Oven cooking chamber.
3. Select "Air Fry" of Iconites Air Fryer Toaster Oven and then adjust the temperature to 380 degrees F.
4. Set the timer for 25 minutes and press "Start" to preheat.
5. After preheating, insert 1 tray in the top position and another in the bottom position of oven.
6. Switch the position of cooking trays once halfway through.
7. Meanwhile, in a small pan, add the remaining ingredients over medium heat and cook for about 10 minutes, stirring occasionally.
8. When cooking time is complete, remove the trays from oven.
9. In a large bowl, add the chicken wings and honey mixture and toss to coat well.
10. Serve immediately.

Nutritional Information per Serving:

- Calories 524
- Total Fat 16.9 g
- Saturated Fat 4.6 g
- Cholesterol 202 mg
- Sodium 534 mg
- Total Carbs 24 g
- Fiber 0.2 g
- Sugar 21.1 g
- Protein 66.2 g

Marinated Chicken Legs

Preparation Time: 15 minutes
Cooking Time: 20 minutes
Servings: 4

Ingredients:

- 4 (8-ounce) chicken legs
- 2 tablespoons balsamic vinegar
- 2 teaspoons garlic, minced
- Salt, as required
- 4 tablespoons plain Greek yogurt
- 1 teaspoon red chili powder
- 1 teaspoon ground cumin
- 1 teaspoon ground coriander
- Ground black pepper, as required

Method:

1. In a bowl, add the chicken legs, vinegar, garlic and salt and mix well.
2. Set aside for about 15 minutes.
3. Meanwhile, in another bowl, mix together the yogurt, spices, salt and black pepper.
4. Add the chicken legs into bowl and coat with the spice mixture generously.
5. Cover the bowl of chicken and refrigerate for at least 10-12 hours.
6. Arrange the chicken legs into the greased basket.
7. Arrange the basket in the center of Iconites Air Fryer Oven.
8. Select "Air Fry" of Iconites Air Fryer Toaster Oven and then adjust the temperature to 445 degrees F.
9. Set the timer for 20 minutes and press "Start" to preheat.
10. After preheating, insert the basket in the oven.
11. When cooking time is complete, remove the basket from oven.
12. Serve hot.

Nutritional Information per Serving:

- Calories 450
- Total Fat 17.2 g
- Saturated Fat 4.8 g
- Cholesterol 203 mg
- Sodium 253 mg
- Total Carbs 2.2 g
- Fiber 0.3 g
- Sugar 1.2 g
- Protein 66.7 g

Glazed Chicken Drumsticks

Preparation Time: 15 minutes
Cooking Time: 20 minutes
Servings: 4

Ingredients:

- ¼ cup Dijon mustard
- 1 tablespoon honey
- 2 tablespoons canola oil
- 1 tablespoon fresh parsley, minced
- Salt and ground black pepper, as required
- 4 (6-ounce) chicken drumsticks

Method:

1. Marinated the chicken drumsticks with all the above ingredients for overnight. Preheat Philips Airfryer at 160 degree. In bowl, add all ingredients except the drumsticks and mix until well combined.
2. Add the drumsticks and coat with the mixture generously.
3. Cover the bowl and place in the refrigerator to marinate overnight.
4. Place the chicken drumsticks into the greased baking pan.
5. Select "Air Fry" of Iconites Air Fryer Oven and then adjust the temperature to 320 degrees F.
6. Set the timer for 12 minutes and press Start to preheat.
7. After preheating, insert the baking pan in the oven.
8. After 12 minutes, flip the drumsticks and set the temperature to 390 degrees F for 8 minutes.
9. When cooking time is complete, remove the chicken drumsticks from oven and serve hot.

Nutritional Information per Serving:

- Calories 376
- Total Fat 17.4 g
- Saturated Fat 3.1 g
- Cholesterol 150 mg
- Sodium 353 mg
- Total Carbs 5.2 g
- Fiber 0.6 g
- Sugar 4.5 g
- Protein 47.5 g

Breaded Chicken Breasts

Preparation Time: 15 minutes
Cooking Time: 12 minutes
Servings: 6

Ingredients:

- 1 cup breadcrumbs
- ½ cup Parmesan cheese, grated
- ¼ cup fresh parsley, minced
- Salt and ground black pepper, as required
- 1½ pounds boneless, skinless chicken breasts
- 3 tablespoons olive oil
- Olive oil cooking spray

Method:

1. In a shallow dish, add the breadcrumbs, Parmesan cheese, parsley, salt and black pepper mix well.
2. Rub the chicken breasts with oil and then, coat with the breadcrumbs mixture evenly.
3. Arrange the chicken breasts onto a baking pan and spray with cooking spray.
4. Arrange the drip pan in the bottom of Instant Iconites Air Fryer Oven cooking chamber.
5. Select "Air Fry" of Iconites Air Fryer Toaster Oven and then adjust the temperature to 350 degrees F.
6. Set the timer for 12 minutes and press "Start" to preheat.
7. After preheating, insert the cooking pan in the center position of oven.
8. Flip the chicken breasts once halfway through.
9. When cooking time is complete, remove the chicken breasts and serve hot.

Nutritional Information per Serving:

- Calories 371
- Total Fat 18 g
- Saturated Fat 4.3 g
- Cholesterol 106 mg
- Sodium 315 mg
- Total Carbs 13.1 g
- Fiber 0.9 g
- Sugar 1.1 g
- Protein 38 g

Buttered Turkey Breast

Preparation Time: 15 minutes
Cooking Time: 55 minutes
Servings: 6

Ingredients:

- ¼ cup butter, softened
- 4 tablespoons fresh rosemary, chopped
- Salt and ground black pepper, as required
- 1 (4-pound) bone-in, skin-on turkey breast
- 2 tablespoons olive oil

Method:

1. In a bowl, add the butter, rosemary, salt and black pepper and mix well.
2. Rub the herb mixture under skin evenly.
3. Coat the outside of turkey breast with oil.
4. Place the turkey breast into the greased baking pan.
5. Select "Bake" of Iconites Air Fryer Oven and then adjust the temperature to 350 degrees F.
6. Set the timer for 55 minutes and press "Start" to preheat.
7. After preheating, insert the baking pan in the oven.
8. When cooking time is complete, remove the turkey breast from oven and place onto a cutting board.
9. With a piece of foil, cover the turkey breast for about 20 minutes before slicing.
10. With a sharp knife, cut the turkey breast into desired-sized slices and serve.

Nutritional Information per Serving:

- Calories 628
- Total Fat 34.3 g
- Saturated Fat 11.1 g
- Cholesterol 209 mg
- Sodium 461 mg
- Total Carbs 1.4 g
- Fiber 0.9 g
- Sugar 0 g
- Protein 65 g

Herbed Turkey Breast

Preparation Time: 15 minutes
Cooking Time: 1 hour
Servings: 8

Ingredients:

- 2 tablespoons olive oil
- 2 tablespoons lemon juice
- 1 tablespoon garlic, minced
- 2 teaspoons ground mustard
- Salt and ground black pepper, as required
- 1 teaspoon ground sage
- 1 teaspoon dried thyme
- 1 teaspoon dried rosemary
- 1 (3-pound) turkey breast

Method:

1. In a small bowl, add all the ingredients except the turkey breast and mix until well combined.
2. Rub the oil mixture on the outside of the turkey breast and under any loose skin generously.
3. Arrange the turkey breast onto a cooking tray, skin side up.
4. Arrange the drip pan in the bottom of Instant Iconites Air Fryer Oven cooking chamber.
5. Select "Air Fry" of Iconites Air Fryer Toaster Oven and then adjust the temperature to 360 degrees F.
6. Set the timer for 60 minutes and press "Start" to preheat.
7. After preheating, insert the cooking tray in the center position of oven.
8. When cooking time is complete, press the red lever to release the rod.
9. Remove from the oven and place the turkey breast onto a platter for about 5-10 minutes before slicing.
10. With a sharp knife, cut the turkey breast into desired sized slices and serve.

Nutritional Information per Serving:

- Calories 214
- Total Fat 6.6 g
- Saturated Fat 1.1 g
- Cholesterol 73 mg
- Sodium 800 mg
- Total Carbs 8.1 g
- Fiber 1.2 g
- Sugar 6.1 g
- Protein 29.4 g

Garlicky Duck Legs

Preparation Time: 10 minutes
Cooking Time: 30 minutes
Servings: 2

Ingredients:

- 2 garlic cloves, minced
- 1 tablespoon fresh parsley, chopped
- 1 teaspoon five-spice powder
- Salt and ground black pepper, as required
- 2 duck legs

Method:

1. In a bowl, mix add the garlic, parsley, five-spice powder, salt and black pepper and mix until well combined.
2. Rub the duck legs with garlic mixture generously.
3. Arrange the duck legs onto the greased baking pan.
4. Select "Air Fry" of Iconites Air Fryer Oven and then adjust the temperature to 340 degrees F.
5. Set the timer for 30 minutes and press "Start" to preheat.
6. After preheating, insert the baking pan the oven.
7. When cooking time is complete, remove the turkey legs from oven and serve hot.

Nutritional Information per Serving:

- Calories 434
- Total Fat 14.4 g
- Saturated Fat 3.2 g
- Cholesterol 253 mg
- Sodium 339 mg
- Total Carbs 1.1 g
- Fiber 0.1 g
- Sugar 0.1 g
- Protein 70.4 g

Chapter 5: Red Meat Recipes

Bacon-Wrapped Filet Mignon

Preparation Time: 15 minutes
Cooking Time: 15 minutes
Servings: 2

Ingredients:

- 2 bacon slices
- 2 (4-ounce) filet mignon
- Salt and ground black pepper, as required
- Olive oil cooking spray

Method:

1. Wrap 1 bacon slice around each filet mignon and secure with toothpicks.
2. Season the filets with the salt and black pepper lightly.
3. Select "Air Fry" of Iconites Air Fryer Oven and then adjust the temperature to 375 degrees F.
4. Set the timer for 15 minutes and press "Start" to preheat.
5. After preheating, arrange the filets over the greased rack and insert in the oven.
6. Flip the filets once halfway through.
7. When cooking time is complete, remove the rack from oven and serve.

Nutritional Information per Serving:

- Calories 226
- Total Fat 9.5 g
- Saturated Fat 3.6 g
- Cholesterol 79 mg
- Sodium 220 mg
- Total Carbs 0 g
- Fiber 0 g
- Sugar 0 g
- Protein 33.3 g

Lemony Flank Steak

Preparation Time: 15 minutes
Cooking Time: 12 minutes
Servings: 6

Ingredients:

- 2 pounds flank steak
- 3 tablespoons fresh lemon juice
- 2 tablespoons olive oil
- 3 garlic cloves, minced
- 1 teaspoon red chili powder
- Salt and ground black pepper, as required

Method:

1. In a large bowl, add all the ingredients except for steak and mix well.
2. Add the flank steak and coat with the marinade generously.
3. Refrigerate to marinate for 24 hours, flipping occasionally.
4. Arrange the steak onto a greased baking pan.
5. Select "Broil" of Iconites Air Fryer Oven and set the timer for 12 minutes.
6. Press "Start" to preheat.
7. After preheating, insert the baking pan in the top portion of oven.
8. Flip the steak once halfway through.
9. When cooking time is complete, remove the baking pan from oven.
10. Place the roast onto a cutting board for about 10-15 minutes before slicing.
11. With a sharp knife, cut the roast into desired size slices and serve.

Nutritional Information per Serving:

- Calories 339
- Total Fat 17.4 g
- Saturated Fat 6 g
- Cholesterol 83 mg
- Sodium 118 mg
- Total Carbs 0.9 g
- Fiber 0.2 g
- Sugar 0.2 g
- Protein 42.3 g

Seasoned Rib-Eye Steak

Preparation Time: 10 minutes
Cooking Time: 14 minutes
Servings: 3

Ingredients:

- 2 (8-ounce) rib-eye steaks
- 2 tablespoons olive oil
- 1 tablespoon steak seasoning
- Salt and ground black pepper, as required

Method:

1. Coat the steaks with oil and then, sprinkle with seasoning, salt and black pepper evenly.
2. Arrange the steaks onto a baking pan.
3. Select "Steak" of Iconites Air Fryer Oven and then adjust the temperature to 400 degrees F.
4. Set the timer for 14 minutes and press "Start" to preheat.
5. After preheating, insert the baking pan in the oven.
6. When cooking time is complete, remove the steaks from oven and place onto a cutting board for about 5 minutes.
7. Cut each steak into desired sized slices and serve.

Nutritional Information per Serving:

- Calories 495
- Total Fat 42.8 g
- Saturated Fat 14.7 g
- Cholesterol 100 mg
- Sodium 137 mg
- Total Carbs 0 g
- Fiber 0 g
- Sugar 0 g
- Protein 26.8 g

Spicy Beef Chuck Roast

Preparation Time: 10 minutes
Cooking Time: 45 minutes
Servings: 6

Ingredients:

- 1 tablespoon olive oil
- 1 tablespoon smoked paprika
- 1 teaspoon ground cumin
- ½ teaspoon garlic powder
- ½ teaspoon onion powder
- Salt and ground black pepper, as required
- 1 (2-pound) beef chuck roast

Method:

1. In a bowl, add the oil, spices, salt and black pepper and mix well.
2. Coat the beef roast with herb mixture generously.
3. Arrange the beef roast onto the greased baking pan.
4. Select "Air Fry" of Iconites Air Fryer Oven and then adjust the temperature to 360 degrees F.
5. Set the timer for 45 minutes and press "Start" to preheat.
6. After preheating, insert the baking pan in the oven.
7. When cooking time is complete, remove the sirloin roast from oven and place onto a cutting board.
8. With a piece of foil, cover the beef roast for about 20 minutes before slicing.
9. With a sharp knife, cut the beef roast into desired sized slices and serve.

Nutritional Information per Serving:

- Calories 353
- Total Fat 15.1 g
- Saturated Fat 4.9 g
- Cholesterol 153 mg
- Sodium 128 mg
- Total Carbs 1.1 g
- Fiber 0.5 g
- Sugar 0.3 g
- Protein 50.2 g

Seasoned Beef Roast

Preparation Time: 10 minutes
Cooking Time: 45 minutes
Servings: 8

Ingredients:

- 2½ pounds beef roast
- 1 tablespoon olive oil
- 2 tablespoons Montreal steak seasoning

Method:

1. With kitchen twines, tie the roast into a compact shape.
2. Brush the roast with oil and then rub with seasoning.
3. Arrange the beef roast onto a greased baking pan.
4. Select "Air Fry" of Iconites Air Fryer Toaster Oven and then adjust the temperature to 360 degrees F.
5. Set the timer for 45 minutes and press "Start" to preheat.
6. After preheating, arrange the baking pan in the center of oven.
7. When cooking time is complete, remove the baking pan from oven.
8. Place the steak onto a cutting board for about 10-15 minutes before slicing.
9. With a sharp knife, cut the steak into desired sized slices and serve.

Nutritional Information per Serving:

- Calories 283
- Total Fat 10.6 g
- Saturated Fat 3.6 g
- Cholesterol 127 mg
- Sodium 653 mg
- Total Carbs 09 g
- Fiber 0 g
- Sugar 0 g
- Protein 43 g

Herbed Pork Loin

Preparation Time: 10 minutes
Cooking Time: 20 minutes
Servings: 6

Ingredients:

- 3 tablespoons sugar
- 1 teaspoon dried basil
- 1 teaspoon dried thyme
- 1 teaspoon dried rosemary
- 1 teaspoon garlic powder
- Salt and ground black pepper, as required
- 2 pounds pork loin

Method:

1. In a bowl, add the sugar, herbs, garlic powder, salt and black pepper and mix well.
2. Rub the pork loin with bail mixture generously.
3. Place the pork loin into a greased basket.
4. Select "Air Fry" of Iconites Air Fryer Toaster Oven and then adjust the temperature to 400 degrees F.
5. Set the timer for 20 minutes and press "Start" to preheat.
6. After preheating, arrange the basket in the center of oven.
7. When cooking time is complete, remove the basket from oven.
8. Place the pork loin onto a cutting board for about 10 minutes before slicing.
9. With a sharp knife, cut the loin into desired sized slices and serve.

Nutritional Information per Serving:

- Calories 391
- Total Fat 21.1 g
- Saturated Fat 7.9 g
- Cholesterol 121 mg
- Sodium 130 mg
- Total Carbs 6.6 g
- Fiber 0.2 g
- Sugar 6.1 g
- Protein 41.4 g

Glazed Pork Tenderloin

Preparation Time: 15 minutes
Cooking Time: 20 minutes
Servings: 3

Ingredients:

- 1 pound pork tenderloin
- 2 tablespoons Sriracha
- 2 tablespoons honey
- Salt, as required

Method:

1. Insert the rotisserie rod through the pork tenderloin.
2. Insert the rotisserie forks, one on each side of the rod to secure the pork tenderloin.
3. In a small bowl, add the Sriracha, honey and salt and mix well.
4. Brush the pork tenderloin with honey mixture evenly.
5. Arrange the drip pan in the bottom of Instant Iconites Air Fryer Oven cooking chamber.
6. Select "Air Fry" of Iconites Air Fryer Toaster Oven and then adjust the temperature to 350 degrees F.
7. Set the timer for 20 minutes and press "Start" to preheat.
8. After preheating, press the red lever down and load the left side of the rod into the oven.
9. Now, slide the rod's left side into the groove along the metal bar so it doesn't move.
10. Then, close the door and touch "Rotate".
11. When cooking time is complete, press the red lever to release the rod.
12. Remove the pork from oven and place onto a platter for about 10 minutes before slicing.
13. With a sharp knife, cut the roast into desired sized slices and serve.

Nutritional Information per Serving:

- Calories 269
- Total Fat 5.3 g
- Saturated Fat 1.8 g
- Cholesterol 110 mg
- Sodium 207 mg
- Total Carbs 13.5 g
- Fiber 0 g
- Sugar 11.6 g
- Protein 39.7 g

Seasoned Pork Shoulder

Preparation Time: 15 minutes
Cooking Time: 1 hour
Servings: 10

Ingredients:

- 3 pounds skin-on, bone-in pork shoulder
- 2-3 tablespoons adobo seasoning
- Salt, as required

Method:

1. Arrange the pork shoulder onto a cutting board, skin-side down.
2. Season the inner side of pork shoulder with adobo seasoning and salt.
3. Season the inner side of pork shoulder with salt and adobo seasoning
4. With kitchen twines, tie the pork shoulder into a long round cylinder shape.
5. Season the outer side of pork shoulder with salt.
6. Insert the rotisserie rod through the pork shoulder.
7. Insert the rotisserie forks, one on each side of the rod to secure the pork shoulder.
8. Arrange the drip pan in the bottom of Iconites Air Fryer Oven.
9. Now, slide the rod's left side into the groove along the metal bar so it doesn't move.
10. Then, close the door and touch "Rotate".
11. Select "Roast" of Iconites Air Fryer Oven and then adjust the temperature to 350 degrees F.
12. Set the timer for 60 minutes and press "Start" to preheat.
13. When cooking time is complete, press the red lever to release the rod.
14. Remove the pork from oven and place onto a platter for about 10 minutes before slicing.
15. With a sharp knife, cut the pork shoulder into desired sized slices and serve.

Nutritional Information per Serving:

- Calories 397
- Total Fat 29.1 g
- Saturated Fat 10.7 g
- Cholesterol 122 mg
- Sodium 176 mg
- Total Carbs 0 g
- Fiber 0 g
- Sugar 0 g
- Protein 31.7 g

Herbed Pork Chops

Preparation Time: 15 minutes
Cooking Time: 12 minutes
Servings: 4

Ingredients:

- 2 garlic cloves, minced
- ½ tablespoon fresh rosemary, chopped
- ½ tablespoon fresh parsley, chopped
- 2 tablespoons olive oil
- ¾ tablespoon Dijon mustard
- 1 tablespoon ground cumin
- 1 teaspoon sugar
- Salt and ground black pepper, as required
- 4 (6-ounces) (1-inch thick) pork chops

Method:

1. In a bowl, mix together the garlic, herbs, oil, mustard, cumin, sugar, and salt.
2. Add the pork chops and generously coat with marinade.
3. Cover the bowl and refrigerate for about 2-3 hours.
4. Remove the chops from the refrigerator and set aside at room temperature for about 30 minutes.
5. Arrange the chops onto the greased baking pan.
6. Select "Air Fry" of Iconites Air Fryer Oven and then adjust the temperature to 390 degrees F.
7. Set the timer for 12 minutes and press "Start" to preheat.
8. After preheating, insert the baking pan in the oven.
9. Flip the chops once halfway through.
10. When cooking time is complete, remove the chops from oven and serve hot.

Nutritional Information per Serving:

- Calories 323
- Total Fat 21.5 g
- Saturated Fat 6.5 g
- Cholesterol 97 mg
- Sodium 515 mg
- Total Carbs 3 g
- Fiber 0.5 g
- Sugar 1.1 g
- Protein 32.5 g

Pork Stuffed Bell Peppers

Preparation Time: 20 minutes
Cooking Time: 1 hour 10 minutes
Servings: 4

Ingredients:

- 4 medium green bell peppers
- 2/3 pound ground pork
- 2 cups cooked white rice
- 1½ cups marinara sauce, divided
- 1 teaspoon Worcestershire sauce
- 1 teaspoon Italian seasoning
- Salt and ground black pepper, as required
- ½ cup mozzarella cheese, shredded

Method:

1. Cut the tops from bell peppers and then carefully remove the seeds.
2. Heat a large skillet over medium heat and cook the pork for bout 6-8 minutes, breaking into crumbles.
3. Add the rice, ¾ cup of marinara sauce, Worcestershire sauce, Italian seasoning, salt and black pepper and stir to combine.
4. Remove from the heat.
5. Arrange the bell peppers into the greased baking pan.
6. Carefully, stuff each bell pepper with the pork mixture and top each with the remaining sauce.
7. Select "Bake" of Iconites Air Fryer Toaster Oven and then adjust the temperature to 350 degrees F.
8. Set the timer for 60 minutes and press "Start" to preheat.
9. After preheating, insert the baking pan in oven.
10. After 50 minute of cooking, top each bell pepper with cheese.
11. When cooking time is complete, remove the baking pan from oven.
12. Serve warm.

Nutritional Information per Serving:

- Calories 580
- Total Fat 7.1 g
- Saturated Fat 2.2 g
- Cholesterol 60 mg
- Sodium 509 mg
- Total Carbs 96.4 g
- Fiber 5.2 g
- Sugar 14.8 g
- Protein 30.3 g

Rosemary Leg of Lamb

Preparation Time: 15 minutes
Cooking Time: 1 hour 40 minutes
Servings: 10

Ingredients:

- ¼ cup olive oil
- 4 garlic cloves, chopped
- ¼ cup fresh rosemary
- 3 tablespoons Dijon mustard
- 2 tablespoons maple syrup
- Salt and ground black pepper, as required
- 1 (4-pound) leg of lamb

Method:

1. In a food processor, add the oil, garlic, herbs, mustard, honey, salt and black pepper and pulse until smooth.
2. Place the leg of lamb and marinade into a glass baking dish and mix well
3. With plastic wrap, cover the baking dish and refrigerate to marinate for 6-8 hours.
4. Arrange a wire rack in a baking pan.
5. Arrange the leg of lamb into the prepared baking pan.
6. Arrange the drip pan in the bottom of Iconites Air Fryer Oven.
7. Place the baking pan over the drip pan.
8. Select "Bake" of Iconites Air Fryer Oven and then adjust the temperature to 420 degrees F.
9. Set the timer for 20 minutes and press "Start" to preheat.
10. After preheating, insert the baking pan in the center position of oven.
11. After 20 minutes, set the temperature to 320 degrees F for 1 hour and 20 minutes.
12. When cooking time is complete, remove the baking pan from oven.
13. Place the leg of lamb onto a cutting board.
14. With a piece of foil, cover the leg of lamb for about 10 minutes before slicing.
15. With a sharp knife, cut the leg of lamb into desired size slices and serve.

Nutritional Information per Serving:

- Calories 401
- Total Fat 18.8 g
- Saturated Fat 5.6 g
- Cholesterol 163 mg
- Sodium 208 mg
- Total Carbs 4.3 g
- Fiber 0.8 g
- Sugar 2.4 g
- Protein 51.3 g

Glazed Lamb Meatballs

Preparation Time: 20 minutes
Cooking Time: 30 minutes
Servings: 8

Ingredients:

For Meatballs:

- 2 pounds lean ground lamb
- 2/3 cup quick-cooking oats
- ½ cup Ritz crackers, crushed
- 1 (5-ounce) can evaporated milk
- 2 large eggs, beaten lightly
- 1 teaspoon maple syrup
- 1 tablespoon dried onion, minced
- Salt and ground black pepper, as required

For Sauce:

- 1/3 cup orange marmalade
- 1/3 cup maple syrup
- 1/3 cup sugar
- 2 tablespoons cornstarch
- 2 tablespoons soy sauce
- 1-2 tablespoons Sriracha
- 1 tablespoon Worcestershire sauce

Method:

1. For meatballs: in a large bowl, add all the ingredients and mix until well combined.
2. Make 1½-inch balls from the mixture.
3. Arrange half of the meatballs onto the greased baking pan in a single layer.
4. Select "Air Fry" of Iconites Air Fryer Toaster Oven and then adjust the temperature to 380 degrees F.
5. Set the timer for 15 minutes and press "Start" to preheat.
6. After preheating, insert the baking pan in the oven.
7. Flip the meatballs once halfway through.
8. When cooking time is complete, remove the baking pan from oven and transfer the meatballs into a bowl.
9. Repeat with the remaining meatballs.
10. Meanwhile, for sauce: in a small pan, add all the ingredients over medium heat and cook until thickened, stirring continuously.
11. Serve the meatballs with the topping of sauce.

Nutritional Information per Serving:

- Calories 413
- Total Fat 11.9 g
- Saturated Fat 4.3 g
- Cholesterol 145 mg
- Sodium 423 mg
- Total Carbs 39.5 g
- Fiber 1 g
- Sugar 28.2 g
- Protein 36.2 g

Crusted Rack of Lamb

Preparation Time: 15 minutes
Cooking Time: 19 minutes
Servings: 4

Ingredients:

- 1 rack of lamb, trimmed all fat and frenched
- Salt and ground black pepper, as required
- 1/3 cup pistachios, chopped finely
- 2 tablespoons panko breadcrumbs
- 2 teaspoons fresh thyme, chopped finely
- 1 teaspoon fresh rosemary, chopped finely
- 1 tablespoon butter, melted
- 1 tablespoon Dijon mustard

Method:

1. Insert the rotisserie rod through the rack on the meaty side of the ribs, right next to the bone.
2. Insert the rotisserie forks, one on each side of the rod to secure the rack.
3. Season the rack with salt and black pepper evenly.
4. Arrange the drip pan in the bottom of Instant Iconites Air Fryer Oven cooking chamber.
5. Select "Air Fry" of Iconites Air Fryer Toaster Oven and then adjust the temperature to 380 degrees F.
6. Set the timer for 12 minutes and press "Start" to preheat.
7. After preheating, press the red lever down and load the left side of the rod into the Oven.
8. Now, slide the rod's left side into the groove along the metal bar so it doesn't move.
9. Then, close the door and touch "Rotate".
10. Meanwhile, in a small bowl, mix together the remaining ingredients except the mustard.
11. When cooking time is complete, press the red lever to release the rod.
12. Remove the rack from oven and brush the meaty side with the mustard.
13. Then, coat the pistachio mixture on all sides of the rack and press firmly.
14. Now, place the rack of lamb onto a baking pan, meat side up.
15. Select "Air Fry" of Iconites Air Fryer Toaster Oven and adjust the temperature to 380 degrees F.

16. Set the timer for 7 minutes and press "Start" to preheat.
17. After preheating, insert the baking pan in the center position of oven.
18. When cooking time is complete, remove the baking pan from oven and place the rack onto a cutting board for at least 10 minutes.
19. Cut the rack into individual chops and serve.

Nutritional Information per Serving:

- Calories 824
- Total Fat 39.3 g
- Saturated Fat 14.2 g
- Cholesterol 233 mg
- Sodium 373 mg
- Total Carbs 10.3 g
- Fiber 1.2 g
- Sugar 0.2 g
- Protein 72 g

Sweet & Soup Lamb Chops

Preparation Time: 15 minutes
Cooking Time: 40 minutes
Servings: 3

Ingredients:

- 3 (8-ounce) lamb shoulder chops
- Salt and ground black pepper, as required
- ¼ cup brown sugar
- 2 tablespoons fresh lemon juice

Method:

1. Season the lamb chops with salt and black pepper generously.
2. In a baking pan, place the chops and sprinkle with sugar, followed by the lime juice.
3. Arrange the drip pan in the bottom of Iconites Air Fryer Oven.
4. Select "Bake" of Iconites Air Fryer Oven and then adjust the temperature to 376 degrees F.
5. Set the timer for 40 minutes and press "Start" to preheat.
6. After preheating, place the baking pan over the drip pan and insert in the oven.
7. Flip the chops once halfway through.
8. When cooking time is complete, remove the baking pan from oven.
9. Serve hot.

Nutritional Information per Serving:

- Calories 390
- Total Fat 18.1 g
- Saturated Fat 6.1 g
- Cholesterol 151 mg
- Sodium 216 mg
- Total Carbs 12.1 g
- Fiber 0 g
- Sugar 11.9 g
- Protein 44.3 g

Lamb Burgers

Preparation Time: 15 minutes
Cooking Time: 8 minutes
Servings: 6

Ingredients:

- 2 pounds ground lamb
- 1 tablespoon onion powder
- Salt and ground black pepper, as required

Method:

1. In a bowl, add all the ingredients and mix well.
2. Make 6 equal-sized patties from the mixture.
3. Arrange the patties onto a wire rack.
4. Arrange the drip pan in the bottom of Instant Iconites Air Fryer Oven cooking chamber.
5. Select "Air Fry" of Iconites Air Fryer Toaster Oven and then adjust the temperature to 360 degrees F.
6. Set the timer for 8 minutes and press "Start" to preheat.
7. After preheating, insert the wire rack in the center position of oven.
8. Flip the burgers once halfway through.
9. When cooking time is complete, remove the rack from Oven and serve hot.

Nutritional Information per Serving:

- Calories 285
- Total Fat 11.1 g
- Saturated Fat 4 g
- Cholesterol 136 mg
- Sodium 143 mg
- Total Carbs 0.9 g
- Fiber 0.1 g
- Sugar 0.4 g
- Protein 42.6 g

Chapter 6: Seafood Recipes

Buttered Salmon

Preparation Time: 10 minutes
Cooking Time: 10 minutes
Servings: 2

Ingredients:

- 2 (6-ounces) salmon fillets
- Salt and ground black pepper, as required
- 1 tablespoon butter, melted

Method:

1. Season each salmon fillet with salt and black pepper and then, coat with the butter.
2. Arrange the salmon fillets onto the greased baking pan in a single layer.
3. Select "Air Fry" of Iconites Air Fryer Oven and then adjust the temperature to 360 degrees F.
4. Set the timer for 12 minutes and press "Start" to preheat.
5. After preheating, insert the baking pan in the oven.
6. When cooking time is complete, remove the fish fillets from oven and serve hot.

Nutritional Information per Serving:

- Calories 276
- Total Fat 16.3 g
- Saturated Fat 5.2 g
- Cholesterol 90 mg
- Sodium 193 mg
- Total Carbs 0 g
- Fiber 0 g
- Sugar 0 g
- Protein 33.1 g

Lemony Salmon

Preparation Time: 15 minutes
Cooking Time: 10 minutes
Servings: 2

Ingredients:

- 1 tablespoon fresh lemon juice
- ½ tablespoons olive oil
- Salt and ground black pepper, as required
- 1 garlic clove, minced
- ½ teaspoon fresh thyme leaves, chopped
- 2 (7-ounce) salmon fillets

Method:

1. In a bowl, add all the ingredients except the salmon and mix well.
2. Add the salmon fillets and coat with the mixture generously.
3. Coat the fillets with flour mixture, then dip into egg mixture and finally coat with the cornflake mixture.
4. Arrange the salmon fillets onto a lightly greased wire rack, skin-side down.
5. Arrange the drip pan in the bottom of Instant Iconites Air Fryer Oven cooking chamber.
6. Select "Air Fry" of Iconites Air Fryer Toaster Oven and then adjust the temperature to 400 degrees F.
7. Set the timer for 10 minutes and press "Start" to preheat.
8. After preheating, insert the wire rack in the bottom position of oven.
9. Flip the fillets once halfway through.
10. When cooking time is complete, remove the track from oven and serve hot.

Nutritional Information per Serving:

- Calories 297
- Total Fat 15.8 g
- Saturated Fat 2.3 g
- Cholesterol 88 mg
- Sodium 167 mg
- Total Carbs 0.8 g
- Fiber 0.2 g
- Sugar 0.2 g
- Protein 38.7 g

Breaded Cod

Preparation Time: 15 minutes
Cooking Time: 10 minutes
Servings: 4

Ingredients:

- 1/3 cup all-purpose flour
- Ground black pepper, as required
- 1 large egg
- 2 tablespoons water
- 2/3 cup cornflakes, crushed
- 1 tablespoon Parmesan cheese, grated
- 1/8 teaspoon cayenne pepper
- 1 pound cod fillets
- Salt, as required

Method:

1. Put the flour and black pepper in a shallow dish and mix well.
2. In a second shallow dish, add the egg and water and beat well.
3. In a third shallow dish, add the cornflakes, cheese and cayenne pepper. and mix well.
4. Season the cod fillets with salt evenly.
5. Coat the fillets with flour mixture, then dip into egg mixture and finally coat with the cornflake mixture.
6. Arrange the cod fillets onto a wire rack.
7. Arrange the drip pan in the bottom of Instant Iconites Air Fryer Oven cooking chamber.
8. Select "Air Fry" of Iconites Air Fryer Toaster Oven and then adjust the temperature to 400 degrees F.
9. Set the timer for 10 minutes and press "Start" to preheat.
10. After preheating, insert the wire rack in the bottom position of oven.
11. Flip the cod fillets once halfway through.
12. When cooking time is complete, remove the rack from oven and serve hot.

Nutritional Information per Serving:

- Calories 168
- Total Fat 2.7 g
- Saturated Fat 0.6 g
- Cholesterol 103 mg
- Sodium 172 mg
- Total Carbs 12.1 g
- Fiber 0.5g
- Sugar 0.6 g
- Protein 23.7 g

Spiced Tilapia

Preparation Time: 15 minutes
Cooking Time: 12 minutes
Servings: 2

Ingredients:

- ½ teaspoon lemon pepper seasoning
- ½ teaspoon garlic powder
- 1/2 teaspoon onion powder
- Salt and ground black pepper, as required
- 2 (6-ounce) tilapia fillets
- 1 tablespoon olive oil

Method:

1. In a small bowl, mix together the spices, salt and black pepper.
2. Coat the tilapia fillets with oil and then rub with spice mixture.
3. Arrange the salmon fillets onto a lightly greased wire rack, skin-side down.
4. Arrange the drip pan in the bottom of Instant Iconites Air Fryer Oven cooking chamber.
5. Select "Air Fry" of Iconites Air Fryer Toaster Oven and then adjust the temperature to 360 degrees F.
6. Set the timer for 12 minutes and press "Start" to preheat.
7. After preheating, insert the wire rack in the bottom position of oven.
8. Flip the fillets once halfway through.
9. When cooking time is complete, remove the rack from oven and serve hot.

Nutritional Information per Serving:

- Calories 206
- Total Fat 8.6 g
- Saturated Fat 1.7 g
- Cholesterol 83 mg
- Sodium 138 mg
- Total Carbs 0.2 g
- Fiber 0.2 g
- Sugar 0.4 g
- Protein 31.9 g

Breaded Hake

Preparation Time: 15 minutes
Cooking Time: 12 minutes
Servings: 4

Ingredients:

- 1 egg
- 4 ounce breadcrumbs
- 2 tablespoons vegetable oil
- 4 (6-ounce) hake fillets
- 1 lemon, cut into wedges

Method:

1. In a shallow bowl, whisk the egg.
2. In another bowl, add the breadcrumbs and oil and mix until a crumbly mixture forms.
3. Dip fish fillets into the egg and then, coat with the breadcrumbs mixture.
4. Arrange the hake fillets in greased basket.
5. Select "Air Fry" of Iconites Air Fryer Toaster Oven and then adjust the temperature to 350 degrees F.
6. Set the timer for 12 minutes and press "Start" to preheat.
7. After preheating, insert the basket in oven.
8. When cooking time is complete, remove the basket from oven.
9. Serve hot.

Nutritional Information per Serving:

- Calories 297
- Total Fat 10.6 g
- Saturated Fat 2 g
- Cholesterol 89 mg
- Sodium 439 mg
- Total Carbs 22 g
- Fiber 1.4 g
- Sugar 1.9 g
- Protein 29.2 g

Trout with Broccoli

Preparation Time: 15 minutes
Cooking Time: 12 minutes
Servings: 2

Ingredients:

- 1 cup small broccoli florets
- 2 tablespoons olive oil, divided
- Salt and ground black pepper, as required
- ½ teaspoon fresh ginger, grated
- 1 tablespoon soy sauce
- 1 teaspoon fresh lime juice
- 1 teaspoon brown sugar
- ¼ teaspoon cornstarch
- 2 (6-ounce) trout fillets
- 1 scallion, thinly sliced

Method:

1. In a bowl, mix together the broccoli, 1 tablespoon of oil, salt, and black pepper.
2. In another bowl, add the ginger, soy sauce, lime juice, brown sugar, and cornstarch and mix until well combined.
3. Coat the trout fillets with remaining oil and then with the ginger mixture.
4. Arrange the broccoli florets into the greased air frying basket and top with the trout fillets.
5. Select "Air Fry" of Iconites Air Fryer Oven and then adjust the temperature to 375 degrees F.
6. Set the timer for 12 minutes and press "Start" to preheat.
7. After preheating, insert the basket in the oven.
8. When cooking time is complete, remove the basket from oven and serve hot

Nutritional Information per Serving:

- Calories 474
- Total Fat 28.6 g
- Saturated Fat 4.5 g
- Cholesterol 126 mg
- Sodium 582 mg
- Total Carbs 6.3 g
- Fiber 1.5 g
- Sugar 2.6 g
- Protein 47.3 g

Halibut & Shrimp with Pasta

Preparation Time: 15 minutes
Cooking Time: 18 minutes
Servings: 4

Ingredients:

- 14 ounces pasta
- 4 tablespoons pesto, divided
- 4 (4-ounce) halibut steaks
- 2 tablespoons olive oil
- ½ pound tomatoes, chopped
- 8 large shrimp, peeled and deveined
- 2 tablespoons fresh lime juice
- 2 tablespoons fresh dill, chopped

Method:

1. In the bottom of a baking pan, spread 1 tablespoon of pesto.
2. Place halibut steaks and tomatoes over pesto in a single layer and drizzle with the oil.
3. Now, place the shrimp on top in a single layer.
4. Drizzle with lime juice and sprinkle with dill.
5. Select "Air Fry" of Iconites Air Fryer Oven and then adjust the temperature to 390 degrees F.
6. Set the timer for 8 minutes and press "Start" to preheat.
7. After preheating, place the baking pan over the rack and insert in the oven.
8. Meanwhile, in a large pan of salted boiling water, add the pasta and cook for about 8-10 minutes or until desired doneness.
9. Drain the pasta and transfer into a large bowl.
10. Add the remaining pesto and toss to coat well.
11. When cooking time is complete, remove the pan from oven.
12. Divide the pasta onto serving plate and top with fish mixture.
13. Serve immediately.

Nutritional Information per Serving:

- Calories 606
- Total Fat 19.4 g
- Saturated Fat 3.2 g
- Cholesterol 205 mg
- Sodium 294 mg
- Total Carbs 59.1 g
- Fiber 1.1 g
- Sugar 2.5 g
- Protein 47.4 g

Lemony Shrimp

Preparation Time: 15 minutes
Cooking Time: 8 minutes
Servings: 3

Ingredients:

- 2 tablespoons fresh lemon juice
- 1 tablespoon olive oil
- 1 teaspoon lemon pepper
- ¼ teaspoon paprika
- ¼ teaspoon garlic powder
- 12 ounces medium shrimp, peeled and deveined

Method:

1. In a large bowl, add all the ingredients except the shrimp and mix until well combined.
2. Add the shrimp and toss to coat well.
3. Arrange the shrimps onto a cooking tray.
4. Arrange the drip pan in the bottom of Instant Iconites Air Fryer Oven cooking chamber.
5. Select "Air Fry" of Iconites Air Fryer Toaster Oven and then adjust the temperature to 400 degrees F.
6. Set the timer for 8 minutes and press "Start" to preheat.
7. After preheating, insert the wire rack in the center position of oven.
8. When cooking time is complete, remove the tray from oven and serve hot.

Nutritional Information per Serving:

- Calories 154
- Total Fat 6.1 g
- Saturated Fat 0.8 g
- Cholesterol 2230 mg
- Sodium 259 mg
- Total Carbs 0.9 g
- Fiber 0.3 g
- Sugar 0.3 g
- Protein 24.5 g

Herbed Scallops

Preparation Time: 15 minutes
Cooking Time: 4 minutes
Servings: 2

Ingredients:

- ¾ pound sea scallops, cleaned and pat dry
- 1 tablespoon butter, melted
- ¼ tablespoon fresh thyme, minced
- ¼ tablespoon fresh rosemary, minced
- Salt and ground black pepper, as required

Method:

1. In a large bowl, place the scallops, butter, herbs, salt, and black pepper and toss to coat well.
2. Arrange the scallops into the greased basket.
3. Select "Air Fry" of Iconites Air Fryer Toaster Oven and then adjust the temperature to 390 degrees F.
4. Set the timer for 4 minutes and press "Start" to preheat.
5. After preheating, insert the basket in the oven.
6. When cooking time is complete, remove the basket from oven and serve hot.

Nutritional Information per Serving:

- Calories 203
- Total Fat 7.1 g
- Saturated Fat 3.8 g
- Cholesterol 71 mg
- Sodium 393 mg
- Total Carbs 4.5 g
- Fiber 0.3 g
- Sugar 0 g
- Protein 28.7 g

Crab Cakes

Preparation Time: 15 minutes
Cooking Time: 10 minutes
Servings: 4

Ingredients:

- ¼ cup red bell pepper, seeded and chopped finely
- 2 scallions, chopped finely
- 2 tablespoons mayonnaise
- 2 tablespoons breadcrumbs
- 1 tablespoon Dijon mustard
- 1 teaspoon old bay seasoning
- 8 ounces lump crabmeat, drained

Method:

1. In a large bowl, add all the ingredients except crabmeat and mix until well combined.
2. Gently fold in the crabmeat.
3. Make 4 equal-sized patties from the mixture.
4. Arrange the patties onto a lightly greased wire rack.
5. Arrange the drip pan in the bottom of Iconites Air Fryer Toaster Oven cooking chamber.
6. Select "Air Fry" of Iconites Air Fryer Toaster Oven and then adjust the temperature to 370 degrees F.
7. After preheating, insert the rack in the center position of oven.
8. When cooking time is complete, remove the rack from oven and serve hot.

Nutritional Information per Serving:

- Calories 91
- Total Fat 7.4 g
- Saturated Fat 0.4 g
- Cholesterol 34 mg
- Sodium 603 mg
- Total Carbs 6.4 g
- Fiber 0.6 g
- Sugar 1.3 g
- Protein 9.1 g

Chapter 7: Vegan Recipes

Brussels Sprout Salad

Preparation Time: 15 minutes
Cooking Time: 15 minutes
Servings: 4

Ingredients:

For Salad:

- 1 pound fresh medium Brussels sprouts, trimmed and halved vertically
- 3 teaspoons olive oil
- Salt and ground black pepper, as required
- 2 apples, cored and chopped
- 1 red onion, sliced
- 4 cups lettuce, torn

For Dressing:

- 2 tablespoons extra-virgin olive oil
- 2 tablespoons fresh lemon juice
- 1 tablespoon apple cider vinegar
- 1 tablespoon maple syrup
- 1 teaspoon Dijon mustard
- Salt and ground black pepper, as required

Method:

1. For Brussels sprout: in a bowl, add the Brussels sprout, oil, salt, and black pepper and toss to coat well.
2. Spread the Brussels sprouts onto a baking pan.
3. Select "Air Fry" of Iconites Air Fryer Toaster Oven and then adjust the temperature to 360 degrees F.
4. Set the timer for 15 minutes and press "Start" to preheat.
5. After preheating, insert the baking pan in the oven.
6. Flip the Brussels sprout once halfway through.
7. When cooking time is complete, remove the baking pan from oven.
8. Transfer the Brussel sprouts onto a plate and set aside to cool slightly.
9. In a serving bowl, mix together the Brussel sprouts, apples, onion, and lettuce.
10. For dressing: in a bowl, add all the ingredients and beat until well combined.
11. Place the dressing over salad and gently, stir to combine.

12. Serve immediately.

Nutritional Information per Serving:

- Calories 235
- Total Fat 11.3 g
- Saturated Fat 1.7 g
- Cholesterol 0 mg
- Sodium 88 mg
- Total Carbs 34.5 g
- Fiber 8 g
- Sugar 20.3 g
- Protein 4.9 g

Basil Tomatoes

Preparation Time: 10 minutes
Cooking Time: 10 minutes
Servings: 2

Ingredients:

- 3 tomatoes, halved
- Olive oil cooking spray
- Salt and ground black pepper, as required
- 1 tablespoon fresh basil, chopped

Method:

1. Drizzle cut sides of the tomato halves with cooking spray evenly.
2. Sprinkle with salt, black pepper and basil.
3. Arrange the tomatoes in the basket.
4. Select "Air Fry" of Iconites Air Fryer Toaster Oven and then adjust the temperature to 320 degrees F.
5. Set the timer for 10 minutes and press "Start" to preheat.
6. After preheating, insert the basket in oven.
7. When cooking time is complete, remove the basket from oven serve warm.

Nutritional Information per Serving:

- Calories 34
- Total Fat 0.4 g
- Saturated Fat 0.1 g
- Cholesterol 0 mg
- Sodium 87 mg
- Total Carbs 7.2 g
- Fiber 2.2 g
- Sugar 4.9 g
- Protein 1.7 g

Spicy Potatoes

Preparation Time: 15 minutes
Cooking Time: 25 minutes
Servings: 4

Ingredients:

- 2 cups water
- 6 russet potatoes, peeled and cubed
- ½ tablespoon extra-virgin olive oil
- ½ of onion, chopped
- 1 tablespoon fresh rosemary, chopped
- 1 garlic clove, minced
- 1 jalapeño pepper, chopped
- ½ teaspoon garam masala powder
- ¼ teaspoon ground cumin
- ¼ teaspoon red chili powder
- Salt and ground black pepper, as required

Method:

1. In a large bowl, add the water and potatoes and set aside for about 30 minutes.
2. Drain well and pat dry with the paper towels.
3. In a bowl, add the potatoes and oil and toss to coat well.
4. Arrange the potato cubes in the basket.
5. Select "Air Fry" of Iconites Air Fryer Toaster Oven and then adjust the temperature to 330 degrees F.
6. Set the timer for 5 minutes and press "Start" to preheat.
7. After preheating, insert the basket in oven.
8. When cooking time is complete, remove the basket from oven and transfer the potatoes into a bowl.
9. Add the remaining ingredients and toss to coat well.
10. Again, arrange the potato cubes in the basket.
11. Select "Air Fry" of Iconites Air Fryer Toaster Oven and then adjust the temperature to 390 degrees F.
12. Set the timer for 20 minutes and press "Start" to preheat.
13. After preheating, insert in the basket in the oven.
14. When cooking time is complete, remove the basket from oven and serve hot.

Nutritional Information per Serving:

- Calories 274
- Total Fat 2.3 g
- Saturated Fat 0.4 g
- Cholesterol 0 mg

- Sodium 65mg
- Total Carbs 52.6 g
- Fiber 8.5 g
- Sugar 4.4 g
- Protein 5.7 g

Almond Asparagus

Preparation Time: 10 minutes
Cooking Time: 6 minutes
Servings: 3

Ingredients:

- 1 pound asparagus
- 2 tablespoons olive oil
- 2 tablespoons balsamic vinegar
- Salt and ground black pepper, as required
- 1/3 cup almonds, sliced

Method:

1. In a bowl, mix together the asparagus, oil, vinegar, salt, and black pepper.
2. Arrange the veggie mixture in greased "Air Fry Basket"
3. Select "Air Fry" of Iconites Air Fryer Toaster Oven and then adjust the temperature to 400 degrees F.
4. Set the timer for 6 minutes and press "Start" to preheat.
5. After preheating, insert the basket in oven.
6. When cooking time is complete, remove the basket from oven and serve hot.

Nutritional Information per Serving:

- Calories 173
- Total Fat 14.8 g
- Saturated Fat 1.8 g
- Cholesterol 0 mg
- Sodium 54 mg
- Total Carbs 8.2 g
- Fiber 4.5 g
- Sugar 3.3 g
- Protein 5.6 g

Glazed Carrots

Preparation Time: 15 minutes
Cooking Time: 12 minutes
Servings: 4

Ingredients:

- 3 cups carrots, peeled and cut into large chunks
- 1 tablespoon olive oil
- 1 tablespoon maple syrup
- 1 tablespoon fresh parsley, minced
- Salt and ground black pepper, as required

Method:

1. In a bowl, add the carrot, oil, maple syrup, thyme, salt, and black pepper.
2. Arrange the carrot chunks into the greased basket in a single layer.
3. Select "Air Fry" of Iconites Air Fryer Toaster Oven and then adjust the temperature to 390 degrees F.
4. Set the timer for 12 minutes and press "Start" to preheat.
5. After preheating, insert the basket in the center position of oven.
6. Flip the carrot chunks once halfway through.
7. When cooking time is complete, remove the basket from oven and serve hot.

Nutritional Information per Serving:

- Calories 77
- Total Fat 3.5 g
- Saturated Fat 0.5 g
- Cholesterol 0 mg
- Sodium 97 mg
- Total Carbs 11.5 g
- Fiber 2.1 g
- Sugar 7.1 g
- Protein 0.7 g

Spiced Zucchini

Preparation Time: 10 minutes
Cooking Time: 12 minutes
Servings: 3

Ingredients:

- 1 pound zucchini, cut into ½-inch thick slices lengthwise
- 1 tablespoon olive oil
- ½ teaspoon garlic powder
- ½ teaspoon cayenne pepper
- Salt and ground black pepper, as required

Method:

1. In a bowl, add all the ingredients and toss to coat well.
2. Arrange the zucchini slices onto a baking pan.
3. Select "Air Fry" of Iconites Air Fryer Toaster Oven and then adjust the temperature to 400 degrees F.
4. Set the timer for 12 minutes and press "Start" to preheat.
5. After preheating, insert the baking pan in the center position of oven.
6. When cooking time is complete, remove the pan from oven and serve hot.

Nutritional Information per Serving:

- Calories 67
- Total Fat 5 g
- Saturated Fat 0.7 g
- Cholesterol 0 mg
- Sodium 66 mg
- Total Carbs 5.6 g
- Fiber 1.8 g
- Sugar 2.8 g
- Protein 2 g

Sweet & Tangy Mushrooms

Preparation Time: 10 minutes
Cooking Time: 15 minutes
Servings: 4

Ingredients:

- ¼ cup soy sauce
- ¼ cup maple syrup
- ¼ cup balsamic vinegar
- 2 garlic cloves, chopped finely
- ½ teaspoon red pepper flakes, crushed
- 18 ounces cremini mushrooms, halved

Method:

1. In a bowl, place the soy sauce, honey, vinegar, garlic and red pepper flakes and mix well. Set aside.
2. Place the mushroom into the greased baking pan in a single layer.
3. Select "Bake" of Iconites Air Fryer Toaster Oven and then adjust the temperature to 350 degrees F.
4. Set the timer for 15 minutes and press "Start" to preheat.
5. After preheating, insert the baking pan in oven.
6. After 8 minutes of cooking, place the honey mixture in baking pan and toss to coat well.
7. Serve hot.

Nutritional Information per Serving:

- Calories 113
- Total Fat 0.2 g
- Saturated Fat 0 g
- Cholesterol 0 mg
- Sodium 9.8 mg
- Total Carbs 24.7 g
- Fiber 1 g
- Sugar 20 g
- Protein 4.4 g

Spicy Butternut Squash

Preparation Time: 15 minutes
Cooking Time: 20 minutes
Servings: 4

Ingredients:

- 1 medium butternut squash, peeled, seeded and cut into chunk
- 2 teaspoons cumin seeds
- 1/8 teaspoon garlic powder
- 1/8 teaspoon red pepper flakes, crushed
- Salt and ground black pepper, as required
- 1 tablespoon olive oil
- 2 tablespoons pine nuts
- 2 tablespoons fresh cilantro, chopped

Method:

1. In a bowl, mix together the squash, spices, and oil.
2. Arrange the squash chunks in greased basket.
3. Select "Air Fry" of Iconites Air Fryer Toaster Oven and then adjust the temperature to 375 degrees F.
4. Set the timer for 20 minutes and press "Start" to preheat.
5. After preheating, insert the basket in oven.
6. When cooking time is complete, remove the basket from oven and serve hot with the garnishing of pine nuts and cilantro.

Nutritional Information per Serving:

- Calories 191
- Total Fat 7 g
- Saturated Fat 0.8 g
- Cholesterol 0 mg
- Sodium 52 mg
- Total Carbs 34.3 g
- Fiber 6 g
- Sugar 6.4 g
- Protein 3.7 g

Lemony Okra

Preparation Time: 10 minutes
Cooking Time: 20 minutes
Servings: 2

Ingredients:

- 1 (10-ounce) bag frozen cut okra
- ¼ cup nutritional yeast
- 2 tablespoons fresh lemon juice
- Salt and ground black pepper, as required

Method:

1. In a bowl, add the okra, nutritional yeast, lemon juice, salt, and black pepper and toss to coat well.
2. Arrange the okra into the greased basket in a single layer.
3. Select "Air Fry" of Iconites Air Fryer Oven and then adjust the temperature to 400 degrees F.
4. Set the timer for 20 minutes and press "Start" to preheat.
5. After preheating, insert the basket in the oven.
6. When cooking time is complete, remove the okra from oven and serve hot.

Nutritional Information per Serving:

- Calories 131
- Total Fat 1.5 g
- Saturated Fat 0.3 g
- Cholesterol 0 mg
- Sodium 103 mg
- Total Carbs 20.1 g
- Fiber 9.6 g
- Sugar 2.4 g
- Protein 12.1 g

Seasoned Potatoes

Preparation Time: 10 minutes
Cooking Time: 40 minutes
Servings: 2

Ingredients:

- 2 russet potatoes, scrubbed
- ½ tablespoon olive oil
- ½ teaspoon garlic & herb blend seasoning
- ½ teaspoon garlic powder
- Salt, to taste

Method:

1. In a small bowl, mix together the spices and salt.
2. With a fork, prick the potatoes.
3. Coat the potatoes with butter and sprinkle with spice mixture.
4. Arrange the potatoes into a baking pan.
5. Select "Air Fry" of Iconites Air Fryer Toaster Oven and then adjust the temperature to 400 degrees F.
6. Set the timer for 40 minutes and press "Start" to preheat.
7. After preheating, insert the baking pan in the center position of oven.
8. When cooking time is complete, remove the pan from oven and serve hot.

Nutritional Information per Serving:

- Calories 176
- Total Fat 2.1 g
- Saturated Fat 1.9 g
- Cholesterol 8 mg
- Sodium 111 mg
- Total Carbs 34.2 g
- Fiber 5.2 g
- Sugar 2.6 g
- Protein 3.8 g

Veggie Ratatouille

Preparation Time: 15 minutes
Cooking Time: 15 minutes
Servings: 4

Ingredients:

- 1 green bell pepper, seeded and chopped
- 1 yellow bell pepper, seeded and chopped
- 1 eggplant, chopped
- 1 zucchini, chopped
- 3 tomatoes, chopped
- 2 small onions, chopped
- 2 garlic cloves, minced
- 2 tablespoons Herbs de Provence
- 1 tablespoon olive oil
- 1 tablespoon balsamic vinegar
- Salt and ground black pepper, as required

Method:

1. In a large bowl, add the vegetables, garlic, Herbs de Provence, oil, vinegar, salt, and black pepper and toss to coat well.
2. Transfer vegetable mixture into a greased baking pan.
3. Select "Air Fry" of Iconites Air Fryer Toaster Oven and then adjust the temperature to 355 degrees F.
4. Set the timer for 15 minutes and press "Start" to preheat.
5. After preheating, insert the baking pan in the oven.
6. When cooking time is complete, remove the baking pan from oven and serve hot.

Nutritional Information per Serving:

- Calories 119
- Total Fat 4.2 g
- Saturated Fat 0.6 g
- Cholesterol 0 mg
- Sodium 54 mg
- Total Carbs 20.3 g
- Fiber 7.3 g
- Sugar 11.2 g
- Protein 3.6 g

Tofu with Cauliflower

Preparation Time: 15 minutes
Cooking Time: 1 minutes
Servings: 2

Ingredients:

- ½ (14-ounce) block firm tofu, pressed and cubed
- ½ small head cauliflower, cut into florets
- 1 tablespoon canola oil
- 1 tablespoon nutritional yeast
- ¼ teaspoon dried parsley
- 1 teaspoon ground turmeric
- ¼ teaspoon paprika
- Salt and ground black pepper, as required

Method:

1. In a bowl, mix together the tofu, cauliflower and the remaining ingredients.
2. Arrange the tofu mixture in greased basket.
3. Select "Air Fry" of Iconites Air Fryer Toaster Oven and then adjust the temperature to 390 degrees F.
4. Set the timer for 15 minutes and press "Start" to preheat.
5. After preheating, insert the basket in oven.
6. Flip the tofu mixture once halfway through.
7. When cooking time is complete, remove the basket from oven and serve hot.

Nutritional Information per Serving:

- Calories 170
- Total Fat 11.6 g
- Saturated Fat 1.5 g
- Cholesterol 0 mg
- Sodium 113 mg
- Total Carbs 8.3 g
- Fiber 4.2 g
- Sugar 2.3 g
- Protein 11.9 g

Tofu with Broccoli

Preparation Time: 15 minutes
Cooking Time: 15 minutes
Servings: 3

Ingredients:

- 8 ounces firm tofu, drained, pressed and cubed
- 1 head broccoli, cut into florets
- 1 tablespoon vegetable oil
- 1 teaspoon ground turmeric
- ¼ teaspoon paprika
- Salt and ground black pepper, as required

Method:

1. In a bowl, mix together all ingredients.
2. Place the tofu mixture in the greased baking pan.
3. Select "Air Fry" of Iconites Air Fryer Toaster Oven and then adjust the temperature to 390 degrees F.
4. Set the timer for 15 minutes and press "Start" to preheat.
5. After preheating, insert the baking pan in oven.
6. Toss the tofu mixture once halfway through.
7. When cooking time is complete, remove the pan from oven and serve hot.

Nutritional Information per Serving:

- Calories 119
- Total Fat 7.4 g
- Saturated Fat 3.1 g
- Cholesterol 10 mg
- Sodium 115 mg
- Total Carbs 7.5 g
- Fiber 3.1 g
- Sugar 1.9 g
- Protein 8.7 g

Chapter 8: Snacks Recipes

Spicy Chickpeas

Preparation Time: 5 minutes
Cooking Time: 10 minutes
Servings: 4

Ingredients:

- 1 (15-ounce) can chickpeas, rinsed and drained
- 1 tablespoon olive oil
- ½ teaspoon ground cumin
- ½ teaspoon cayenne pepper
- ½ teaspoon smoked paprika
- Salt, as required

Method:

1. In a bowl, add all the ingredients and toss to coat well.
2. Arrange the chickpeas in a basket.
3. Select "Air Fry" of Iconites Air Fryer Toaster Oven and then adjust the temperature to 390 degrees F.
4. Set the timer for 10 minutes and press "Start" to preheat.
5. After preheating, insert the basket in the oven.
6. When cooking time is complete, remove the basket from oven and set aside to cool slightly.
7. Serve warm.

Nutritional Information per Serving:

- Calories 146
- Total Fat 4.5 g
- Saturated Fat 0.5 g
- Cholesterol 0 mg
- Sodium 66 mg
- Total Carbs 18.8 g
- Fiber 4.6 g
- Sugar 0.1 g
- Protein 6.3 g

Mozzarella Sticks

Preparation Time: 15 minutes
Cooking Time: 12 minutes
Servings: 3

Ingredients:

- 3 tablespoons all-purpose flour
- 2 eggs
- 3 tablespoons milk
- ½ cup breadcrumbs
- ½ pound mozzarella cheese block, cut into 3x½-inch sticks

Method:

1. In a shallow dish, place the flour.
2. In a second shallow dish, add the eggs and milk and beat well.
3. In a third shallow dish, place the breadcrumbs.
4. Coat the Mozzarella sticks with flour, then dip in egg mixture and finally, coat with the breadcrumbs.
5. Arrange the Mozzarella sticks onto a cookie sheet and freeze for about 1-2 hours.
6. Now, place the mozzarella sticks into the greased basket.
7. Arrange the basket in the center of Iconites Air Fryer Oven.
8. Select "Air Fry" of Iconites Air Fryer Toaster Oven and then adjust the temperature to 400 degrees F.
9. Set the timer for 12 minutes and press "Start" to preheat.
10. When cooking time is complete, remove the basket from Oven.
11. Serve warm.

Nutritional Information per Serving:

- Calories 162
- Total Fat 5.1 g
- Saturated Fat 1.8 g
- Cholesterol 113 mg
- Sodium 209 mg
- Total Carbs 20.1 g
- Fiber 1 g
- Sugar 2.1 g
- Protein 8.7 g

Tortilla Chips

Preparation Time: 10 minutes
Cooking Time: 3 minutes
Servings: 3

Ingredients:

- 4 corn tortillas, cut into triangles
- 1 tablespoon olive oil
- Salt, to taste

Method:

1. Coat the tortilla chips with oi and then, sprinkle each side of the tortillas with salt.
2. Arrange the tortilla chips in the basket.
3. Select "Air Fry" of Iconites Air Fryer Toaster Oven and then adjust the temperature to 390 degrees F.
4. Set the timer for 3 minutes and press "Start" to preheat.
5. After preheating, insert the basket in oven.
6. When cooking time is complete, remove the basket from oven and serve warm.

Nutritional Information per Serving:

- Calories 110
- Total Fat 5.6 g
- Saturated Fat 0.8 g
- Cholesterol 0 mg
- Sodium 65 mg
- Total Carbs 14.3 g
- Fiber 2 g
- Sugar 0.3 g
- Protein 1.8 g

Feta Tater Tots

Preparation Time: 15 minutes
Cooking Time: 25 minutes
Servings: 6

Ingredients:

- 2 pounds frozen tater tots
- ½ cup feta cheese, crumbled
- ½ cup tomato, chopped
- ¼ cup black olives, pitted and sliced
- ¼ cup red onion, chopped

Method:

1. Arrange the tater tots in the basket.
2. Select "Air Fry" of Iconites Air Fryer Toaster Oven and then adjust the temperature to 450 degrees F.
3. Set the timer for 15 minutes and press "Start" to preheat.
4. After preheating, insert the basket in oven.
5. When cooking time is complete, remove the basket from oven and transfer tots into a large bowl.
6. Add the feta cheese, tomatoes, olives and onion and toss to coat well.
7. Now, place the mixture into a baking pan.
8. Select "Air Fry" of Iconites Air Fryer Toaster Oven and then adjust the temperature to 450 degrees F.
9. Set the timer for 10 minutes and press "Start" to preheat.
10. After preheating, insert the baking pan in oven.
11. When cooking time is complete, remove the baking pan from oven and serve warm.

Nutritional Information per Serving:

- Calories 322
- Total Fat 17.7 g
- Saturated Fat 5.6 g
- Cholesterol 11 mg
- Sodium 784 mg
- Total Carbs 37.9 g
- Fiber 4.1 g
- Sugar 2 g
- Protein 5.5 g

Jalapeño Poppers

Preparation Time: 15 minutes
Cooking Time: 13 minutes
Servings: 6

Ingredients:

- 12 large jalapeño peppers
- 8 ounces cream cheese, softened
- ¼ cup scallion, chopped
- ¼ cup fresh cilantro, chopped
- ¼ teaspoon onion powder
- ¼ teaspoon garlic powder
- Salt, as required
- 1/3 cup sharp cheddar cheese, grated

Method:

1. Carefully, cut off one-third of each pepper lengthwise and then, scoop out the seeds and membranes.
2. In a bowl, mix together the cream cheese, scallion, cilantro, spices and salt.
3. Stuff each pepper with the cream cheese mixture and top with cheese.
4. Arrange the jalapeño peppers into a greased baking pan.
5. Select "Air Fry" of Iconites Air Fryer Toaster Oven and then adjust the temperature to 400 degrees F.
6. Set the timer for 13 minutes and press "Start" to preheat.
7. After preheating, insert the baking pan in oven.
8. When cooking time is complete, remove the pan from oven and serve immediately.

Nutritional Information per Serving:

- Calories 171
- Total Fat 15.7 g
- Saturated Fat 9.7 g
- Cholesterol 48 mg
- Sodium 914 mg
- Total Carbs 3.7 g
- Fiber 1.3 g
- Sugar 1.2 g
- Protein 4.9 g

Cauliflower Poppers

Preparation Time: 10 minutes
Cooking Time: 20 minutes
Servings: 6

Ingredients:

- 3 tablespoons olive oil
- 1 teaspoon paprika
- ½ teaspoon ground cumin
- ¼ teaspoon ground turmeric
- Salt and ground black pepper, as required
- 1 medium head cauliflower, cut into florets

Method:

1. In a bowl, place all ingredients and toss to coat well.
2. Place the cauliflower mixture in the greased baking pan.
3. Select "Bake" of Iconites Air Fryer Toaster Oven and then adjust the temperature to 450 degrees F.
4. Set the timer for 20 minutes and press "Start" to preheat.
5. After preheating, insert the baking pan in oven.
6. Flip the cauliflower mixture once halfway through.
7. When cooking time is complete, remove the pan from oven and serve warm.

Nutritional Information per Serving:

- Calories 73
- Total Fat 7.1 g
- Saturated Fat 1 g
- Cholesterol 0 mg
- Sodium 41 mg
- Total Carbs 2.7 g
- Fiber 1.3 g
- Sugar 1.1 g
- Protein 1 g

Fish Nuggets

Preparation Time: 15 minutes
Cooking Time: 8 minutes
Servings: 5

Ingredients:

- 1 cup all-purpose flour
- 2 eggs
- ¾ cup seasoned breadcrumbs
- 2 tablespoons vegetable oil
- 1 pound boneless haddock fillet, cut into strips

Method:

1. In a shallow dish, place the flour.
2. In a second dish, crack the eggs and beat well.
3. In a third dish, mix together the breadcrumbs and oil.
4. Coat the nuggets with flour, then dip into beaten eggs and finally, coat with the breadcrumbs.
5. Place the nuggets into the greased basket in a single layer.
6. Select "Air Fry" of Iconites Air Fryer Toaster Oven and then adjust the temperature to 390 degrees F.
7. Set the timer for 8 minutes and press "Start" to preheat.
8. After preheating, insert the basket in the center position of oven.
9. Flip the nuggets once halfway through.
10. When cooking time is complete, remove the basket from oven.
11. Serve warm.

Nutritional Information per Serving:

- Calories 311
- Total Fat 10.4 g
- Saturated Fat 1.7 g
- Cholesterol 110 mg
- Sodium 312 mg
- Total Carbs 29.4 g
- Fiber 1.3 g
- Sugar 0.2 g
- Protein 23.6 g

Buffalo Chicken Wings

Preparation Time: 15 minutes
Cooking Time: 19 minutes
Servings: 4

Ingredients:

- 1½ pounds chicken wings
- 1 teaspoon olive oil
- Salt and ground black pepper, as required
- ¼ cup buffalo sauce

Method:

1. In a large bowl, mix together the chicken wings, oil, salt and black pepper.
2. Arrange the wings into a greased baking pan.
3. Select "Air Fry" of Iconites Air Fryer Toaster Oven and then adjust the temperature to 360 degrees F.
4. Set the timer for 19 minutes and press "Start" to preheat.
5. After preheating, insert the baking pan in oven.
6. Flip the chicken wings once halfway through and coat with buffalo sauce.
7. When cooking time is complete, remove the pan from oven and serve immediately.

Nutritional Information per Serving:

- Calories 334
- Total Fat 13.8 g
- Saturated Fat 3.6 g
- Cholesterol 151 mg
- Sodium 209 mg
- Total Carbs 0.1 g
- Fiber 0 g
- Sugar 0 g
- Protein 49.2 g

Bacon-Wrapped Shrimp

Preparation Time: 15 minutes
Cooking Time: 7 minutes
Servings: 6

Ingredients:

- 1 pound bacon, thinly sliced
- 1 pound shrimp, peeled and deveined

Method:

1. Wrap each shrimp with one bacon slice.
2. Arrange the shrimp in a baking dish and refrigerate for about 20 minutes.
3. Now, place the shrimp into the greased basket.
4. Arrange the basket in the center of Iconites Air Fryer Oven.
5. Select "Air Fry" of Iconites Air Fryer Toaster Oven and then adjust the temperature to 390 degrees F.
6. Set the timer for 7 minutes and press "Start" to preheat.
7. After preheating, insert the baking pan in oven.
8. When cooking time is complete, remove the basket from oven.
9. Serve warm.

Nutritional Information per Serving:

- Calories 499
- Total Fat 32.9 g
- Saturated Fat 10.8 g
- Cholesterol 242 mg
- Sodium 1800 mg
- Total Carbs 2.2 g
- Fiber 0 g
- Sugar 0 g
- Protein 45.2 g

Crispy Coconut Prawns

Preparation Time: 20 minutes
Cooking Time: 12 minutes
Servings: 4

Ingredients:

- ½ cup flour
- ¼ teaspoon paprika
- Salt and ground white pepper, as required
- 2 egg whites
- ¾ cup panko breadcrumbs
- ½ cup unsweetened coconut, shredded
- 2 teaspoons lemon zest, grated finely
- 1 pound prawns, peeled and deveined

Method:

1. In a shallow plate, place the flour, paprika, salt and white pepper and mix well.
2. In a second shallow plate, add the egg whites and beat lightly.
3. In a third shallow plate, place the breadcrumbs, coconut and lemon zest and mix well.
4. Coat the prawns with flour mixture, then dip into egg whites and finally coat with the coconut mixture.
5. Place the prawns into a greased baking pan.
6. Select "Bake" of Iconites Air Fryer Toaster Oven and then adjust the temperature to 400 degrees F.
7. Set the timer for 12 minutes and press "Start" to preheat.
8. After preheating, insert the baking pan in oven.
9. Flip the cauliflower mixture once halfway through.
10. When cooking time is complete, remove the pan from oven and serve hot.

Nutritional Information per Serving:

- Calories 310
- Total Fat 6.9 g
- Saturated Fat 4.1 g
- Cholesterol 239 mg
- Sodium 296 mg
- Total Carbs 18.7 g
- Fiber 1.5 g
- Sugar 0.9 g
- Protein 30.2 g

Chapter 9: Dessert Recipes

Banana Split

Preparation Time: 15 minutes
Cooking Time: 14 minutes
Servings: 8

Ingredients:

- 3 tablespoons coconut oil
- 1 cup panko breadcrumbs
- ½ cup corn flour
- 2 eggs
- 4 bananas, peeled and halved lengthwise
- 3 tablespoons sugar
- ¼ teaspoon ground cinnamon
- 2 tablespoons walnuts, chopped

Method:

1. In a medium skillet, melt the coconut oil over medium heat and cook breadcrumbs for about 3-4 minutes or until golden browned and crumbled, stirring continuously.
2. Transfer the breadcrumbs into a shallow bowl and set aside to cool.
3. In a second bowl, place the corn flour.
4. In a third bowl, whisk the eggs.
5. In a small bowl, mix together the sugar and cinnamon.
6. Coat the banana slices with flour and then, dip into eggs and finally, coat evenly with the breadcrumbs.
7. Arrange the banana slices in a basket and sprinkle with cinnamon sugar.
8. After preheating, insert the basket in the center position of oven.
9. When cooking time is complete, remove the basket from oven.
10. Transfer the banana slices onto plates to cool slightly
11. Sprinkle with chopped walnuts and serve.

Nutritional Information per Serving:

- Calories 216
- Total Fat 8.8g
- Saturated Fat 5.3 g
- Cholesterol 41 mg
- Sodium 16 mg
- Total Carbs 26 g
- Fiber 2.3 g
- Sugar 11.9 g
- Protein 3.4 g

Glazed Figs

Preparation Time: 10 minutes
Cooking Time: 10 minutes
Servings: 4

Ingredients:

- 4 fresh figs
- 4 teaspoons honey
- 2/3 cup Mascarpone cheese, softened
- Pinch of ground cinnamon

Method:

1. Cut each fig into the quarter, leaving just a little at the base to hold the fruit together.
2. Arrange the figs onto parchment paper lined baking pan and drizzle with honey.
3. Place about 2 teaspoons of Mascarpone cheese in the center of each fig and sprinkle with cinnamon.
4. Select "Broil" of Iconites Air Fryer Oven and set the timer for 15 minutes.
5. Press "Start" to preheat.
6. After preheating, insert the baking pan in the top portion of oven.
7. When cooking time is complete, remove the pan from oven and serve warm.

Nutritional Information per Serving:

- Calories 141
- Total Fat 5.5 g
- Saturated Fat 3.5 g
- Cholesterol 21 mg
- Sodium 37 mg
- Total Carbs 19.2 g
- Fiber 1.9 g
- Sugar 15 g
- Protein 5.3 g

Lime Mousse

Preparation Time: 15 minutes
Cooking Time: 12 minutes
Servings: 2

Ingredients:

- 4 ounces cream cheese, softened
- ½ cup heavy cream
- 2 tablespoon fresh lime juice
- 5-6 drops liquid stevia
- Pinch of salt

Method:

1. In a bowl, add all the ingredients and mix until well combined.
2. Transfer the mixture into 2 ramekins.
3. Arrange a sheet pan in the center of Iconites Air Fryer Oven.
4. Place the ramekins over a baking pan.
5. Select "Air Fry" of Iconites Air Fryer Toaster Oven and then adjust the temperature to 350 degrees F.
6. Set the timer for 12 minutes and press "Start" to preheat.
7. After preheating, insert the baking pan in oven.
8. When cooking time is complete, remove the ramekins from oven
9. Place the ramekins onto a wire rack to cool.
10. Refrigerate for at least 3 hours before serving.

Nutritional Information per Serving:

- Calories 302
- Total Fat 30.2 g
- Saturated Fat 19.4 g
- Cholesterol 103 mg
- Sodium 257 mg
- Total Carbs 2.4 g
- Fiber 0 g
- Sugar 0.1 g
- Protein 4.9 g

Egg Soufflé

Preparation Time: 15 minutes
Cooking Time: 30 minutes
Servings: 6

Ingredients:

- ¼ cup butter, softened
- ¼ cup all-purpose flour
- ½ cup plus 2 tablespoons sugar, divided
- 1 cup milk
- 3 teaspoons vanilla extract, divided
- 4 egg yolks
- 5 egg whites
- 1 teaspoon cream of tartar
- 2 tablespoons powdered sugar plus extra for dusting

Method:

1. In a bowl, add the butter and flour and mix until a smooth paste forms.
2. In a medium pan, mix together ½ cup of sugar and milk over medium-low heat and cook for about 3 minutes or until the sugar is dissolved, stirring continuously.
3. Add the flour mixture, whisking continuously and simmer for about 3-4 minutes or until mixture becomes thick.
4. Remove from the heat and stir in 1 teaspoon of vanilla extract.
5. Set aside for about 10 minutes to cool.
6. In a bowl, mix together the egg yolks and 1 teaspoon of vanilla extract.
7. Add the egg yolk mixture into milk mixture and mix until well combined.
8. In another bowl, add the egg whites, cream of tartar, remaining sugar, and vanilla extract and whisk until stiff peaks form.
9. Fold the egg whites mixture into milk mixture.
10. Place mixture into 6 greased ramekins evenly and with the back of a spoon, smooth the top surface.
11. Place the ramekins over a baking pan.
12. Select "Air Fry" of Iconites Air Fryer Toaster Oven and then adjust the temperature to 330 degrees F.
13. Set the timer for 16 minutes and press "Start" to preheat.
14. After preheating, insert the baking pan in the center position of oven.
15. When cooking time is complete, remove the ramekins from oven and place the pan onto a wire rack to cool slightly.

16. Sprinkle with the powdered sugar and serve warm.

Nutritional Information per Serving:

- Calories 255
- Total Fat 11.6 g
- Saturated Fat 6.5 g
- Cholesterol 163 mg
- Sodium 107mg

- Total Carbs 31.2 g
- Fiber 0.1 g
- Sugar 26.4 g
- Protein 6.8 g

Plum Crisp

Preparation Time: 15 minutes
Cooking Time: 40 minutes
Servings: 2

Ingredients:

- 1½ cups plums, pitted and sliced
- ¼ cup sugar, divided
- 1½ teaspoons cornstarch
- 3 tablespoons flour
- ¼ teaspoon ground cinnamon
- Pinch of salt
- 1½ tablespoons cold butter, chopped
- 3 tablespoons rolled oats

Method:

1. In a bowl, place plum slices, 1 teaspoon of sugar and cornstarch and toss to coat well.
2. Divide the plum mixture into lightly greased 2 (8-ounce) ramekins.
3. In a bowl, mix together the flour, remaining sugar, cinnamon and salt.
4. With a pastry blender, cut in bitterer until a crumbly mixture forms.
5. Add the oats and gently, stir to combine.
6. Place the oat mixture over plum slices into each ramekin.
7. Arrange the ramekins over the wire rack.
8. Select "Bake" of Iconites Air Fryer Toaster Oven and then adjust the temperature to 350 degrees F.
9. Set the timer for 40 minutes and press "Start" to preheat.
10. After preheating, insert the wire rack in oven.
11. When cooking time is complete, remove the ramekins from oven and place onto a wire rack to cool for about 10 minutes.
12. Serve warm.

Nutritional Information per Serving:

- Calories 273
- Total Fat 9.4 g
- Saturated Fat 5.6 g
- Cholesterol 23 mg
- Sodium 140 mg
- Total Carbs 47.2 g
- Fiber 1.9 g
- Sugar 30.4 g
- Protein 2.7 g

Fruity Crumble

Preparation Time: 15 minutes
Cooking Time: 20 minutes
Servings: 4

Ingredients:

- ½ pound apple, peeled, cored and cubed
- 1 cup fresh blueberries
- 1/3 cup sugar, divided
- 1 tablespoon fresh lemon juice
- 7/8 cup all-purpose flour
- Pinch of salt
- 1 tablespoon cold water
- ¼ cup chilled butter, cubed

Method:

1. Grease a baking pan.
2. In a large bowl, add apricots, blueberries, 2 tablespoons of sugar and lemon juice and mix well.
3. Place the fruit mixture into the prepared baking pan.
4. In another bowl, add the flour, remaining sugar, salt, water, and butter and mix until a crumbly mixture forms.
5. Spread the flour mixture over fruit mixture evenly.
6. Arrange the baking pan over the wire rack.
7. Select "Air Fry" of Iconites Air Fryer Oven and then adjust the temperature to 390 degrees F.
8. Set the timer for 20 minutes and press "Start" to preheat.
9. After preheating, insert the wire rack in oven.
10. When cooking time is complete, remove the pan from oven and place onto a wire rack to cool for about 10 minutes before serving.

Nutritional Information per Serving:

- Calories 300
- Total Fat 12 g
- Saturated 7.4 g
- Cholesterol 31 mg
- Sodium 122 mg
- Total Carbs 46.7 g
- Fiber 2.3 g
- Sugar 23.3 g
- Protein 3.3 g

Zucchini Mug Cake

Preparation Time: 10 minutes
Cooking Time: 20 minutes
Serving: 1

Ingredients:

- ¼ cup whole-wheat pastry flour
- 1 tablespoon sugar
- ¼ teaspoon baking powder
- ¼ teaspoon ground cinnamon
- Pinch of salt
- 2 tablespoons plus 2 teaspoons milk
- 2 tablespoons zucchini, grated and squeezed
- 2 tablespoons almonds, chopped
- 1 tablespoon raisins
- 2 teaspoons maple syrup

Method:

1. In a bowl, mix together the flour, sugar, baking powder, cinnamon and salt.
2. Add the remaining ingredients and mix until well combined.
3. Place the mixture into a lightly greased ramekin.
4. Arrange the ramekins over the wire rack.
5. Select "Bake" of Iconites Air Fryer Oven and then adjust the temperature to 350 degrees F.
6. Set the timer for 20 minutes and press "Start" to preheat.
7. After preheating, insert the wire rack in oven.
8. When cooking time is complete, remove the ramekin from oven and place onto a wire rack to cool slightly before serving.

Nutritional Information per Serving:

- Calories 310
- Total Fat 7 g
- Saturated Fat 0.9 g
- Cholesterol 3 mg
- Sodium 175 mg
- Total Carbs 57.5 g
- Fiber 3.2 g
- Sugar 27.5 g
- Protein 7.2 g

White Chocolate Cheesecake

Preparation Time: 20 minutes
Cooking Time: 34 minutes
Servings: 6

Ingredients:

- 3 eggs (whites and yolks separated)
- 1 cup white chocolate, chopped
- ½ cup cream cheese, softened
- 2 tablespoons unsweetened cocoa powder
- 2 tablespoons powdered sugar
- ¼ cup raspberry jam

Method:

1. In a bowl, add the egg whites and refrigerate to chill before using.
2. In a microwave-safe bowl, add the chocolate and microwave on high heat for about 2 minutes, stirring after every 30 seconds.
3. In the bowl of chocolate, add the cream cheese and microwave for about 1-2 minutes or until cream cheese melts completely.
4. Remove from microwave and stir in cocoa powder and egg yolks.
5. Remove the egg whites from refrigerator and whisk until firm peaks form.
6. Add 1/3 of the mixed egg whites into cheese mixture and gently, stir to combine.
7. Fold in the remaining egg whites.
8. Place the mixture into a 6-inch cake pan.
9. Arrange the cake pan over a baking pan.
10. Select "Air Fry" of Iconites Air Fryer Toaster Oven and then adjust the temperature to 285 degrees F.
11. Set the timer for 30 minutes and press "Start" to preheat.
12. After preheating, insert the baking pan in the center position of oven.
13. When cooking time is complete, remove the pan from oven and place the pan onto a wire rack to cool completely.
14. Then, refrigerate to chill before serving.
15. Just before serving, dust with the powdered sugar.
16. Spread the jam evenly on top and serve.

Nutritional Information per Serving:

- Calories 299
- Total Fat 18.3 g

- Saturated Fat 10.6 g
- Cholesterol 109 mg
- Sodium 114 mg
- Total Carbs 29.8 g
- Fiber 0.7 g
- Sugar 25.5 g
- Protein 6.3 g

Conclusion

Did you like all the delicious recipes? Using these recipes, you can cook an endless menu in your Iconites Air Fryer toaster oven. If you haven't yet tried and experimented with all of its cooking functions, then now it is the time. This Air fryer oven is the innovation of today that has successfully brought a variety of cooking functions in a single appliance. Imagine, instead of having an electric grill, a dehydrator, a toaster, an air fryer, and an oven separately lying in your kitchen, you will have one single appliance which can do all of that with much efficiency. This 10 in 1 multipurpose Iconites oven is extremely user-friendly and gives its users complete control over both the cooking time and temperature. Give you Air Fryer oven a try and cook all the recipes from this book to enjoy the diversity of flavors and aromas.

www.ingramcontent.com/pod-product-compliance
Lightning Source LLC
Chambersburg PA
CBHW081404070526
44583CB00020B/2674